Archaeology and Ghost Research:
A Relational Entanglement

John G. Sabol

Ghost Excavation Research Center

Archaeology and Ghost Research: A Relational Entanglement
~ John G. Sabol ~

Other books by John Sabol

Ghost Excavator (2007)

Ghost Culture (2007)

Gettysburg Unearthed (2007)

Battlefield Hauntscape (2008)

The Anthracite Coal Region (2008)

The Politics of Presence (2008)

Bodies of Substance, Fragments of Memory (2009)

Phantom Gettysburg (2009)

Digging Deep (2009)

The Re-Haunting(s) of Gettysburg (2010)

The Haunted Theatre (2011)

Ghost Culture Too (2012)

Beyond the Paranormal (2012)

Digging-Up Ghosts (2nd publishing, 2013)

Burnside Bridge (2013)

The Gettysburg Experience (2013)

The Absence Above, A Presence Below (2013)

The Production of Haunted Space (2013)

Centralia, Pennsylvania (2013)

The Ghost Excavation (2013)

The Good Death and the Civil War (2014)

Centralia: A Vision of Ruin (2014)

Altered States: Making the Extraordinary Ordinary Again (2014)

Archaeology and Ghost Research:
A Relational Entanglement

Ghost Excavator Books, Inc ™©

Bedford, Pennsylvania, USA

Archaeology and Ghost Research: A Relational Entanglement
~ John G. Sabol ~

Copyright 2014 by John G. Sabol and Ghost Excavation Books, Inc., Bedford, PA, USA. All rights reserved.

Front cover design by Mary Becker, USA. Front cover photo: John Sabol, USA (St. Nicholas Breaker). Back cover photo: Mary Becker, USA (John Sabol - Bath, UK).

The right of John G. Sabol to be identified as the author of the text concepts has been asserted in accordance with section 77 and 78 of the Copyright, Design & Patent Act 1988.

Warning, the text herein is fully protected by U.S. Federal copyright laws. Federal copyright laws will be vigorously enforced and infringement will be prosecuted to the fullest extent of the law, which can include damages and lawyer's fees to be paid by the infringer of copyright. No part of this book may be reproduced or transmitted in any form or by any means, electronic or mechanical, including photocopying, recording or by any information storage and retrieval system without written permission from the publisher. For additional copyright information contact Ghost Excavation Books, Inc., at ghost.excavation@yahoo.com.

All names and original photos are used with permission and copyrighted by their respective owners.

ISBN-13: 978-1500561628
ISBN-10: 1500561622

Ghost Excavation Books, Inc. ™©
A division of C.A.S.P.E.R. Research Center™©,
Bedford, PA, USA
www.ghostexcavation.com

Archaeology and Ghost Research: A Relational Entanglement
~ John G. Sabol ~

Prologue:

A. Questions and Questioning: Why?

Let's begin at the beginning, before we saunter out and "hunt" those "anomalies". Question: why do we (you) go into the field and investigate haunted locations? Doesn't psychical research tell us we should do this "paranormal thing" in the lab under controlled conditions? But is this what occurs in the real world? Wooffitt (2010) suggests otherwise:

"But anomalous experiences, whatever their nature, are inextricably implicated in precisely the social processes and contexts which cannot be reproduced in laboratory conditions" (2010:73).

She suggests that we **"explore the value of empirical perspectives and theoretical positions more associated with research in the social sciences"** (Ibid: 73).

Is "ghost hunting", then, a form of research in the social sciences? Or, has it blossomed into a pathology of TV "edutainment" in the guise of technological dependence? Shouldn't we be less concerned with process (linking technology to "anomaly"), and become more involved in the field in a different way? Shouldn't we become more social scientists, rather than "technologists"?

Also, shouldn't we be less concerned (or not concerned at all) with "debunking", baseline readings (which baseline is it anyway: a present; a contemporary past; a residual past in the present; an interactive past, etc.), and technological saturation coverage? Shouldn't we become more involved with entangled productions: **"the manner in which interpretative experience is produced" (Tilley 1989:278)?**

Let's question ourselves in terms of a reflexive methodology (Hodder 1997). Let's reconceive the fieldwork we do at haunted locations. Let's ask ourselves (quite honestly):

- Why do we go into the field?
- How do we decide what constitutes fieldwork there?
- Why is a "reveal" a post-production process? And
- Why do we do things in a certain way: both in the field, and in revealing our data in social media?

Archaeology and Ghost Research: A Relational Entanglement
~ John G. Sabol ~

B. Is Meaning "Lost in Translation"?

French philosopher Michel Foucault once commented that:

"People know what they do; they frequently know why they do what they do; but what they don't know is what they do does" (quoted in Dreyfus and Rabinow 1983:187).

Does "ghost hunting", how it is executed in the field, have an effect on others (perhaps "unknown" others)? If it does, what effect(s), and does it matter? As a set of performance practices in the contemporary world (whether this is "investigative" or a form of "edutainment" becomes essential), is there a relevancy to this form of exploring a site, location, or landscape?

If this is a moot point to some (perhaps many in the field), it is still important to encourage people to really consider and look constructively at this "hunting" ("paranormal") world. We should think about and critically examine the basic assumptions, as those shared, taken-for-granted notions "ghost hunters" have, and ask:

- Do these practices contribute to our collective knowledge of the world, reality, and the past? Or, are they mere forms of contemporary entertainment within the trope of popular culture?

We should "dig" into these "hunts", and expose to view (allowing all to clearly see) some of the aspects of these

Archaeology and Ghost Research: A Relational Entanglement
~ John G. Sabol ~

"investigative hunts". Let's start from the position of wanting to spend time in the dark at an abandoned place, or a landscape devoid of visible presence. Let's continue with asking "relevant" ("ghost hunter") questions like: "Is anyone here with us tonight?" or "Can you make the lights blink on this meter, or turn my flashlight on?" Isn't this a strange thing to want to do (or asks "someone", not visibly present, to do)? It is because by doing this, all social context is "lost in translation"!

A number of character elements of this type of fieldwork is worthy of deeper thought and consideration. Some of these include the following:

- The process of induction for newcomers and "ghost hunt" beginners: what does the training involve? Who is qualified to train, if (as many say) "there are no experts"?
- Age and social maturity considerations: what communicative skills are necessary? What knowledge of group dynamics is essential for fieldwork?
- The influence of "social" activities during a typical "ghost hunt" (non-investigative) on documenting and experiencing a haunting?

Another consideration is the influence of physical separation (from the mainstream of social life) during fieldwork. This usually occurs as a "place apart" (and different) from the rest of the world. Does a "ghost hunt"

Archaeology and Ghost Research: A Relational Entanglement
~ John G. Sabol ~

build the essential sense of common purpose and unity for a team in the field (such as those that occur in an archaeological excavation team)?

Do we encounter unity of goal and purpose in a "ghost hunting" team out there in the field? Does this physical separation and isolation lead to some non-investigative or non-scientific practices and behaviors (like "run dude run"; screaming and yelling; or congratulatory "pauses" in the middle of the investigation)? Are investigations, once and done, considered "finished"? You can't say you do scientific fieldwork (just by using tech devices) when some behaviors and practices contradict this in the field!

We must come to understand the landscape of a haunted site as a multidimensional space, an entanglement of various social situations. Haunted space should (must) be considered a social field of memory practices. Given this social construction of haunted space, a further distinction is necessary: social identity within situational performances. This re-configures the investigator's position, and the investigative positioning in this social field.

An investigator in haunted space must be socially flexible, and be in (remain) in a position relative to what happened in the past (not the present). In a haunted place, there is no one investigative performance stance because there may be multiple (layered) haunting situations, each with their own memory field, and historically embedded. This

Archaeology and Ghost Research: A Relational Entanglement
~ John G. Sabol ~

requires fieldwork that is centered on multi-spatial/temporal ethnographies within the same location (and possibly the same space). These constitute different nodes of cultural production within a localized space at the same site location.

At a haunted location, we may find that the place is understood, constructed, remembered, and still utilized in very distinct ways by different individual (or groups of) "ghosts". What materializes in the present, and haunts the spaces of a location, may involve long and multiple histories that percolate on the surface of the contemporary environment.

Hence, a thorough investigation should show different senses of history and sociability. These differences would reflect the different entanglements that were produced in the layers of the haunting environment, illustrating the varied types of practices that were (and some that continue to be) associated with the haunted location.

We must diminish the controlling process and effect of paranormal reality TV, ghost tourism, and the "ghost hunting" trope, ones that are largely based on entertainment, ego, and economics. Anthropologist Laura Nader (1997) reminds us that such a controlling process revolves around clusters of beliefs (such as the still unproven entanglement of technology with the documentation of haunting phenomena). These clusters of

Archaeology and Ghost Research: A Relational Entanglement
~ John G. Sabol ~

beliefs restrict the elaboration of alternative (but normal) constructions of reality, past and present.

They do this by merely offering narrow, binary options (such as paranormal/normal; absence/presence; past/present, etc.). This hinders future endeavors and attempts to "leap the fence" (cf. Sabol 2014) of contemporary "ghost hunting".

The contemporary view of a "paranormal world" through "ghost hunting" indicates a disconnection between research and past reality. They reflect different notions of place, space, and cultural behavior, producing a divide between present and past.

Furthermore, "ghost hunting" assumes an identical set of values, physical in nature (as ambient baseline measurements) that can be used at all haunted sites, without regard for differences in occupational layers and social entanglements, and physical (environmental) alterations through time. This creates both miscommunication (electronic manipulation instead of social interaction), different symbolic values (a measuring device instead of a contextual "trigger" aimed at a particular past situation and/or individuals), and a lack of defining different past baseline physical conditions. This can generate indifference and/or confusion ("silence"= no activity) or conflict (an EVP "get out!"), and irrelevance regarding the contemporary baseline measurements/readings,

Archaeology and Ghost Research: A Relational Entanglement
~ John G. Sabol ~

thus making comparative analysis (a drop in temperature; a rise in EMF, etc.) useless.

What is the purpose of "YOUR" ghost research? Is it to benefit the dead (those who may remain; those who are forgotten to history), or the living (for this entertainment, ego, and economics)? As we work in this field, and in the field, our focus on "living" concerns might become blurred to the existence (and moral code) of our cultural past realities. They will continue to remain out of reach because they are viewed as something "paranormal", and thus beyond the scope of our social concern.

This potential ethical conflict with a haunting presence may itself come back to haunt us. As Meskell (2002) states:

"part of the problem rests with the illusion that the subjects of our research are dead and buried, literally, and that our 'scientific' research goals are paramount".

Is that why "ghost hunters" do think twice when they ask the "spirits" to turn on/off (move or control) an electronic device (especially a "ghost (de)tech device)? Do they think that this sequence of events is scientific, or that a measurement of space (as a baseline reading) is doing a controlled, scientific act?

These types of practices and inquiries become a problem in attitude that many bring to the field of ghost research. They become a methodological habit, doing something

Archaeology and Ghost Research: A Relational Entanglement
~ John G. Sabol ~

without thinking through the consequences merely because it's what "everyone does".

I propose that we change these habitual acts. They are not science. Let's move from technological measurement and demand intervention ("Can you.......?") to social engagements of particular cultural entanglements through relational archaeologies (for more see Sabol 2014).

This type of social intervention, using an archaeological sensibility, alters our attitude toward haunted spaces. Fieldwork at haunted locations, I propose, must be considered within their proper socio-cultural and temporal context. This archaeological re-consideration is two-fold:

- How research and fieldwork are performed (as social dynamics) among the investigators (an ethnography of paranormal field practices); and
- The extent of the use of an "outside" context in field practices: the use (or lack) of contemporary contexts at sites of historical depth.

Both of these considerations involve the limited use and entanglement of contemporary technology, social practices, and beliefs within the layers of haunted space at a location.

Within this type of attitude change to fieldwork, there is the practical use of the archaeological concepts of layers of entanglement, each with their own material/sensory remains to engage (and disengage from the present). These layers (distinguishing one from another) require an ethical use of investigative practices and behaviors.

Such an approach, I propose, better meets (compared to "ghost hunts" and technologically-driven "paranormal" investigations) disciplinary standards of a field of social science that focuses on locations perceived as haunted by past presence. This is because its focus is the cultural contexts of past social entanglements, and not documenting (or "debunking") a paranormal event.

Investigators have certain responsibilities to make practical and ethical commitments to fieldwork <u>before</u> they enter a potential haunted space. This commitment to context and ethics must form a vital part of how they imagine and relate to what remains at these sites, as they enter and share those spaces with others who may remain from the past.

Archaeology and Ghost Research: A Relational Entanglement
~ John G. Sabol ~

Photo 1: Fieldwork at a Haunted Location

Archaeology and Ghost Research: A Relational Entanglement
~ John G. Sabol ~

C- What and Who Represents the Past?

The past usually comes to us indirectly through intermediaries: the historian's pen (as written narrative), the archaeological spade and trowel (as excavation), an illustrator's drawing, the photo essay, and computer graphics (to name a few). This allows one access to a past becoming present, as one form of reality. But is there another more immediate and direct means?

Archaeology and Ghost Research: A Relational Entanglement
~ John G. Sabol ~

Photo 2: The Past Becoming Immediately Present (Winchester, UK, 1969)

Photo 3: The Past Becoming Immediately Present (Cholula, Puebla, Mexico, 1970).

Archaeology and Ghost Research: A Relational Entanglement
~ John G. Sabol ~

Is what is being represented merely an improvement in representation through advances in technology, rather than an increase of knowledge about the past and what remains? And in ghost research, are we fooling ourselves and others about how we represent a haunting, as to the reality of a past manifesting in certain locations?

Representation in ghost research reflects two conflicting concepts:

- What is represented: "Ghost hunting" uses a panoptic representation. A light anomaly could (and does for many in the field) represent a visual image of a "ghost". And a EVP is for many, the voice of a "ghost"; and
- What remains to be represented: past presence is synecdochal, not panoptic. What remains are traces and fragments of a more entangled social world.

The panoptic representations of (potential) "presence" would never be a state of presence that an entity from the past ever saw or experienced. Why use them as indicators of "ghostly" presence? They don't relate to any past entanglements of reality. They lack the context of social relativity because their contemporary relationship is entangled with non-relational technology (for the most part), and a social behavior that did not exist in the past, for the most part ("Can you show us a sign of your presence"; can you make the lights blink", etc).

Archaeology and Ghost Research: A Relational Entanglement
~ John G. Sabol ~

The problem is that these "representative" images of a haunting conform to models of "acceptable" ghost hunting practices, yet are derived from still unproven concepts ("orbs"; "ghost box transmissions"; changes in ambient readings) from previous "ghost hunts" (or paranormal investigations).

So what is being represented is a replication which other "ghost hunters" have represented, as nodal ideas along which many of these manifesting elements cluster. The result is a regress of representation, a panoptic image of a haunting that needs correction and re-working!

Through this replicative representation, these images of haunting phenomenon signify to others that this is the reality of "ghost hunting", thus securing the validity of the images for those who enact this type of fieldwork. This has made the artificiality of these representations immediately apparent to the scientific community, yet largely ignored by ghost hunters and paranormal investigators.

Is this misrepresentation of a haunting related to a lack of "experts", and thus a lack of alternative means to offset these misrepresentations and to document what really is materializing (or potentially materializing) of the past at haunted locations? Is there really this lack of representative experts?

Archaeologists believe they have the authority to interpret, and thus represent, the past (Zimmerman 2001). Are

Archaeology and Ghost Research: A Relational Entanglement
~ John G. Sabol ~

archaeologists the experts ghost research needs? Is archaeology the discipline that can make ghost research a legitimate investigative discipline? As an archaeologist, I propose that we can!

This is because archaeological work represents working with the remains (as trace and fragment) of the past in the present, as they actually exist and are represented in the archaeological record. While doing fieldwork at haunted locations, and using an archaeological sensible and sensitive methodology, we can represent ourselves in a more relational way that resonates with the reality of past entanglements. This can be achieved through "performance excavations", as we work within the context of materializations of past trace and fragmented remains.

One example of this work with trace and fragmented synecdochal contextual representations is the monastic costume or "habit". Might not their appearance (in a haunting) be re-represented by a contemporary "excavation" that uses their "habit" as a form of synecdochic entanglement?

Each monastic order was distinguishable by its distinctive "habit", color being a significant "trigger" (examples: Cistercians wore white "habits"; Augustinians wore grey "habits"). The "habit" and the color represents a synecdochal trace or fragment of what a monk's life (and entanglements) were like. The "habit" and the color made

Archaeology and Ghost Research: A Relational Entanglement
~ John G. Sabol ~

the monk part of a particular community and a religious order.

The synecdochal sign entangled the monk in a specific social order. This entanglement can be represented today as a "performance excavation" (a "ghost excavation"), using the synecdochal signs of "habit" and particular color in a common English haunting (for example) of ghostly monks. I say English haunting because the ghosts of **"phantom monks and silent nuns"** are **"unique to England"** (Ackroyd 2010:4).

This type of haunting would be location-specific (England), culture-specific (religious order), and representational specific (the "habit" of a particular color). Any "excavation" of this type of haunting would thus entail resonating with these spatial, social, and cultural entanglements.

If we include other socio-cultural elements (as "excavating triggers"), such as particular prayers, chanting, or even "silence" depending on the religious order, only strengthens this entanglement between past and present. You would not ask a monk, even a "ghostly" one, who perhaps took a vow of silence, to "say something"! Such a monk has no longing to speak, and they certainly are not aware of any electronic devices. Let's keep the ghostly monk within the entanglement of monastic life, not contemporary life.

Archaeology and Ghost Research: A Relational Entanglement
~ John G. Sabol ~

If "ghosts" are real "dead people" (and not some other phenomenon: psychological, cultural, or other), then resonating with past entanglements, in this particular example a human (monk) and his dress ("habit"), would awaken memory, and initiate interaction. This is given the assumption that a "ghost" is not only "real" but is still a trace of human consciousness (in this case still a "monk").

Isn't this approach (as social entanglements through relational archaeologies) more empathetic and contextual than unproven tech scans or a command (demand) to interact with an unknown device? However, we must be cautious in these empathetic attempts at entangling past and present. As Shanks and Tilley (1993) warn:

"Empathy cannot achieve truly historical creation which relates past and present, holding them together in their difference, in the instant of the historic present" (1993:15).

We cannot fully involve ourselves in complete past entanglements. We are, after all, dealing with traces and fragments in archaeology (and in a haunting). Still, empathetic and immersive situational relational archaeologies (such as the example given above) can help to stimulate and enrich our inquiries into an "excavated" haunted space.

We perform (in effect and affect) a form of participant-observation, as an ethno-archaeological approach that deals with the continuing "afterlife" of past social entanglements. If "ghost excavations" are part of an archaeology of the contemporary past (and I propose that they are), then this fieldwork is about surfaces and assemblages (Harrison 2011), and entanglements (Hodder 2012). As Brown, Harrison, and Piccini (2013) suggest:

"We begin as participants, rather than excavators. Different participatory approaches are possible, including what we might call interventions….participation in events….and engagement with communities" (2013:16).

Robert Wlodarski, an archaeologist who has managed and administered more than 300 archaeological and historical projects for a variety of federal and private sector agencies, discusses this "intervention", using past performance and context as a baseline:

"A discussion of ghosts or hauntings will always involve a physical backdrop like a set in a movie replete with costumes and make-up. It will also entail a script where spectral performers act out their scenes….the context (history, time, and location) provides the establishing point for understanding the phenomena; without it, we are truly at a loss for an explanation as to why certain people 'remain behind'" (Wlodarski and Wlodarski 1997:26).

What follows is a re-orientation of contemporary archaeological site performance to engage with and intervene in the continuing entanglement of these past

Archaeology and Ghost Research: A Relational Entanglement
~ John G. Sabol ~

performances, as they emerge and materialize in the present.

Archaeology and Ghost Research: A Relational Entanglement
~ John G. Sabol ~

Table of Contents

Prologue.. 05

   A. Questions and Questioning: Why?.................. 05
   B. Is Meaning "Lost in Translation?"................. 07
   C. What and Who Represents the Past?.............. 16

Table of Contents... 26

Photographs... 28

   1. Introduction: Why Archaeology?...................... 30
      A. The Changing Role of Archaeology and the Archaeological Performance................. 30
      B. The "Active" Ruin that "Haunts": Transforming the Investigative Role...................... 47
      C. Consideration and Intent: An Archaeological Orientation... 50
   2. The Entanglement: Archaeology and Ghost Research.. 53
      A. The Open Past... 53
      B. Travel, Archaeology, and Those Who Remain... 55
      C. The Imprint of Entanglement..................... 59
   3. Haunting Entanglements..................................... 62
      A. A Haunting as Entanglement..................... 62
      B. The Haunting as Actant............................. 67
   4. The Entanglement: Haunted Sites.................... 69
      A. Haunted Sites: Their Temporality not their "Para-History"... 69

Archaeology and Ghost Research: A Relational Entanglement
~ John G. Sabol ~

      B. Haunted Space... 73
      C. The "Hosts" and the "Ghosts"............. 79
  5. Excavating the Entanglement..................... 84
      A. The Entangled Archaeological "Ghost Culture".. 84
      B. Relational Archaeologies and the Haunted Site... 94
      C. Animating a Haunted Site...................... 100
  6. Summary... 102
      A. The Contemporary and Future Relevance and Relation of a "Ghost Excavation"......... 102
      B. The Cardinal Rule: What/"Who" Remains is "Heritage".. 105

Appendix.. 110

  Haunted Houses as Relational Archaeologies.. 110

Bibliography.. 115

Biography.. 125

Archaeology and Ghost Research: A Relational Entanglement
~John G. Sabol ~

Photographs

1. Fieldwork at a Haunted Location................ 15
2. The Past Becoming Immediately Present (Winchester, UK, 1969)............................. 17
3. The Past Becoming Immediately Present (Cholula, Puebla, Mexico, 1970)............................. 18
4. A "Ghost Excavation" Resonating Experience... 38
5. Social Entanglement in a "Ghost Excavation".. 40
6. A "Traditional" Excavation (Cholula, Puebla, Mexico, 1970)....................................... 45
7. A "Ghost Excavation"- Burnside Bridge, Antietam Battlefield, Maryland, USA-2012)................ 46
8. A Haunting Location................................ 63
9. Is This an Entangled Haunted Site............. 66
10. An Entangled Archaeological Landscape....... 72
11. Is This Residual the "Host" or the "Ghost"? (Burnside Bridge, Antietam Battlefield, Maryland).. 83
12. A "Ghost Excavation"............................. 87
13. The "Excavation" of the Daniel Lady Farm (Gettysburg, Pennsylvania)..................... 90
14. Daniel Lady Farm "Excavation"................ 91
15. Daniel Lady Farm "Excavation"................ 92
16. A "Ghost Excavation"............................. 97
17. A "Haunted" Heritage Site...................... 106

Archaeology and Ghost Research: A Relational Entanglement
~ John G. Sabol ~

18. Another "Haunted" Heritage Site............. 109
19. What are the Layers of Entanglement Here?. 114
20. Photo of the Author, John Sabol.................. 125

Archaeology and Ghost Research: A Relational Entanglement
~ John G. Sabol ~

1. ## Introduction: Why Archaeology?

"Where does archaeology stand in relation to all this....in short, why archaeology?"

- Christopher Tilley (1989)

A. ## The Changing Role of Archaeology and the Archaeological Performance

"In summoning the past, we work as shamans: We bring the dead to life; we make them present, and they come to speak to us".

- Alfredo Gonzalez Ruibal (2014:11)

In a forward to *Archaeological Perspectives on the American Civil War* (Geier and Potter 2000), Jim Lehrer says the following:

"We ordinary mortals walk a piece of ground today where a Civil War battle was fought and hear birds singing or breezes blowing through the trees. Archaeologists and anthropologists hear cannon volleys and screams from one hundred and forty years ago" (Geier and Potter 2000: XV).

Are these worded soundings merely the use of the "archaeological imagination" (Shanks 2012), a narrative in archaeological storytelling, or is there something more

Archaeology and Ghost Research: A Relational Entanglement
~ John G. Sabol ~

here? I say, let us look to the archaeological record and observe, as Gavin Lucas (2013) suggests, **"something that gives us access to unfamiliar, new types of entities" (2013:374).** He states that **"we *already* know humans exist: we *already* know pots and arrowheads exist. What does archaeology show us that we did *not* know already?"(Ibid: 374).** Can archaeology be the discipline of new materializations other than "artifacts" (such as pots, "potsherds", and arrowheads)? Can we document the "real" potter behind the "artifact" of the pot?

Can we unearth, through "excavating" performances, something, perhaps "someone", that allows us access to a sensorial experience of the past that we didn't encounter before? Can we excavate "familiar" remains as an unfamiliar recovery? Are these (can these) remains (be) **"vibrant" (Bennett 2010)**? Is there a continuing "life force" in the reality of an excavation, as we "dig-up" the past?

There are places that have the power to frighten, places that are associated with ghosts, the apparitions of the dead. Some of these places are not associated with haunted houses, but with ruins. Anthropologist Gaston Gordillo, doing fieldwork on the Gran Chaco Plains of Northwest Argentina, talks about the ruins of Esteco, as they are perceived by the inhabitants of the nearby town of El Vencido.

Archaeology and Ghost Research: A Relational Entanglement
~ John G. Sabol ~

According to Gordillo (2009), people in El Vencido agree that **"it is possible to hear reverberations of the town's past life"**, and one of his informants stated that **"you heard they were talking, you heard dogs, everything, it was a town"** (2009:346).

This is a place that 'frightens', and it is not centered on one social group. Gordillo states that **"people of diverse class and social backgrounds share the view…"** (Ibid: 347). Local stories indicate a relational entanglement between ghostly presences and local ruins. That these ruins contain human bones only reinforces this association. It:

"creates an apprehension that often resurrects those long-vanished social actors, not as passive objects of remembrance, but as forces embued with agency: as ghosts" (Ibid: 349).

Here, we see objects (ruins) given agency ("ghosts") and thus, a relationship of entanglement is established. Does this show that from what happened in history there is still meaningful presences from the past? Do these ruins have presence? What is important to this continuing entanglement is not the presence of bones, or the vision of what is left (the ruin), but the entanglement between the space and what happened (happens) there. Fear is tied to the space:

"Fear is an embodied articulation of the memories that turn those places in ruins into unstable,

Archaeology and Ghost Research: A Relational Entanglement
~ John G. Sabol ~

discomforting configurations….history is not simply the past but a….forceful presence that still haunts the living" (Gordillo 2009:350).

The landscape becomes an entanglement between particular spaces, structures, social memory, and the manifestation of ghosts. Does this make archaeology, which is the science of such entanglements, a baseline for the investigation and exploration of places perceived to be haunted?

Is archaeology relevant to ghost research? If archaeology is a form of performance practice at sites of abandonment, decay, and ruin, can it unearth what haunts us at these locations? Since archaeology is an entangled part of the present and modern culture, archaeology can filter through to affect various aspects of culture. But can it also affect, and be affected by, a "cultural" haunting? Can an ethnographic approach, such as participant-observation, as part of a "performance excavation" unearth the dead? Anthropologist Clifford Geertz says this:

"It is the anthropologist's particular calling to study the different modes of being human; only by understanding the particulars of these forms of life that we shall find out what it is, or can be, to be human" (1973:53).

Does this include the cultural "afterlife" of human behavior? Can an ethno-archaeological approach, using participation and performance, reach out and include the

Archaeology and Ghost Research: A Relational Entanglement
~ John G. Sabol ~

documentation of this cultural "afterlife" at locations perceived to be haunted? Archaeology does not work with all the past, but what is left of the past in the present, its traces and fragments. Isn't that a haunting? It has been said that archaeology *is* about links between the present and the past, an entanglement between excavation and performance (cf. Shanks and Tilley 1987).

Was Lucas's remarks a statement or a challenge (or both) to expand the field of archaeological exploration? If, as Lucas suggests, that archaeology is the science of new things (2013:378), may these "new" things include buildings as entities? Can they also include, within the frame of habitation (be it house or landscape), other entities, more ephemeral and usually visibly absent, such as a "ghost"? And if we look at a haunted site, as an archaeologist, is there another kind of entity beyond the "ghost", as someone once living but now the "afterlife" of a cultural being? If archaeology is the science of material remains from the past (the science of "things"), why not use its sensibility in exploring what "haunts" us from that past?

Lucas (2012) has re-worked the notion of archaeological entities. The outcome is entity assemblages that, as Jones and Alberti (2013) suggest, are **"in constant flux, assembling and disassembling, materializing and dematerializing…." (2013:29)**. And within this process of entanglement and assemblage, the archaeologist is centered:

Archaeology and Ghost Research: A Relational Entanglement
~ John G. Sabol ~

"Archaeologists are situated within the changing assemblage, and they are only part of what gives it its shape" (Ibid: 29).

Archaeology and the archaeological role is one of relational intervention. This is a participatory-observing mode of operation. There is no prior distinction between the object of study, and the methods we use to observe. There is no separation between past and present. There is entanglement. We cannot describe and understand what remains of the past without acting upon it, and thus shaping the interaction.

This archaeological process, this intervention, is what we must do at a "haunting" site: entangle ourselves in specific practices which shape (recover) what remains (and what materializes). We do this through "excavating" performances. We cannot assign, nor assume, that a site is "haunted" (still "occupied") by the contemporary presence of the past. We also cannot relegate what materializes as something one assumes is "paranormal" in nature. If our acts shape the contemporary archaeological record at a "haunting" site, then what emerges cannot be something beyond our understanding, or beyond normal reality.

A haunting materialization becomes a trace or fragmented assemblage, as its character and affect shifts from one grouping (an entanglement in the past) and set of relationships (past social interaction) to that of another (a contemporary entanglement and present day social

Archaeology and Ghost Research: A Relational Entanglement
~John G. Sabol~

interaction). This is expanding the past toward the future (a present actuality). It is taking a present step back, as we enter a relational process of entanglement <u>before</u> its emergence in the present.

This is not a question of ascertaining or a denial of its existence (the past in the present), as a "debunking" of the haunting. It is a means to ascertain and question the condition (the entangled and relational aspects) of its materialization in the present. It is also not about "ignoring" the "subject", as many skeptics would do.

Our investigative role, albeit an archaeological one, is a responsible one, as we become a productive part of that materializing entangled haunting assemblage. This also involves understanding our involvement at the level of transforming contemporary reality. It is an intervention that affects reality, the way we conceive our fieldwork. It involves relational archaeologies between the experiences of past peoples and what archaeologists do, and how they conduct themselves in the field.

One recent trend in archaeological work, albeit through the use of the archaeological imagination (cf. Shanks 2012), are performance practices aimed at understanding the rhythms of past human activity, such as replicative experiments (Mathieu 2002).

This involves an attempt to recreate past realities (or past situations) in the present, using contemporary performance as analogy with which to answer questions of

Archaeology and Ghost Research: A Relational Entanglement
~ John G. Sabol ~

past activity in the archaeological record. This is to base past processes of production and social entanglements in a specific spacial-temporal context, relating past sequences of cultural activity to actual physical materializations in an archaeological record.

In a "ghost excavation", we take this ethnographic experimentation one step further. We use performance practices, in specific past physical spaces, in an attempt to unearth what remains of past "interactive" activity.

"An archaeologist is a man who knows….that from the surface of rubbish heaps the thin and ghostly essence of things human keeps rising through the centuries until the plaintive murmur of dead men and women may take precedence at times over the living voice. A man who has once looked with the archaeological eye will never see quite normally".

- **Loren Eiseley,** *The Night Country (1972:81).*

Archaeology and Ghost Research: A Relational Entanglement
~ John G. Sabol ~

Photo 4: A "Ghost Excavation" Resonating Experiment

Archaeology and Ghost Research: A Relational Entanglement
~ John G. Sabol ~

Culture is a key concept, I propose, for haunted locations. It is a participatory phenomenon that was (perhaps is) continuously constructed, experienced, and remembered by people. Cultural making and social entanglement, as a process, is a central concept and focus of research in archaeology (Pauketat and Loren 2005).

Archaeology and Ghost Research: A Relational Entanglement
~ John G. Sabol ~

Photo 5: Social Entanglement in a "Ghost Excavation"

Archaeology and Ghost Research: A Relational Entanglement
~ John G. Sabol ~

Cultural entanglements were experienced by people through their **"continuous and historically contingent enactments or embodiments of....attitudes, agendas, and dispositions" (Pauketat 2000:115)**. And these enactments and embodiments **"are routinely recovered by archaeology...." (Emerson and Pauketat 1997:168)**.

But is culture more than material remains? Are ephemeral material (or sensory elements) like residual recordings cultural in nature? Is a haunting, the sense of ghostly presence a cultural phenomenon, something beyond its pop culture connotations? If ghosts exist, do they exhibit past cultural behaviors? The context and content of this book is based on affirmations to these questions.

My (archaeological) work at "haunting" locations is a form of an archaeology that is after interpretation (cf. Jones and Alberti 2013), the cultural meaning behind these materializations. It is hoped that this work is fieldwork **"that exemplifies the current state of archaeological theory" (Jones and Alberti 2013:31)**. These authors state the following:

"In the spirit of becoming, we expect our positions to radically change in the future, just as we anticipate our arguments and materials to be taken up and assembled in novel ways" (Ibid: 31).

Archaeology and Ghost Research: A Relational Entanglement
~John G. Sabol~

A haunted site, I propose, like an archaeological site "targeted" for survey and/or excavation, **"did not have much of a life** (an "afterlife") ....**before they were discovered in their present context" (Holtorf 2008:161).** Materializations that surface, in both a haunting and in archaeology, I propose, may mean (and be) different things to different people.

What is the meaning of material (or sensory) remains to a folklorist, a museum curator, a heritage manager, or a "ghost hunter", or a skeptic? What remains at an archaeological site, or a haunting location, can have parallel "afterlives" in various contemporary contexts and social situations, and within varying moments of recovery (or discovery)?

What are the present archaeological "afterlife" stories? Are they significantly different in meaning to those unearthed in a "ghost excavation"? Is context the deciding factor in making a difference or similarity?

Julian Thomas (1996) has said that to do archaeology, we must recognize certain things as representing evidence. And we must do archaeology in a certain way which enables entities to be recognized.

In a similar way, we must do research and fieldwork in a particular way at a haunted location in order to recognize a haunting materialization. This certain way, I propose, is through relational archaeologies and social entanglements, not tech measurements, EVP scans, or monitoring a

Archaeology and Ghost Research: A Relational Entanglement
~ John G. Sabol ~

darkened space, waiting for something to happen. This certain way, in both archaeology and a "ghost excavation", begins and ends with human (not machine) field performances!

If all presents (and correspondingly all realities) are made of a variety of pasts (Witmore 2007), why not use these relational archaeological entanglements to study and unearth their presences in the present? This should be the future (in the present) of ghost research. And:

"There is only future if we understand its genealogies and if we care for the past – for its spectres, which are not just ethereal beings, but also material remnants that dwell in place" (Gonzalez-Ruibal 2013:22).

These genealogies constitute relational archaeologies, a beneficial entanglement between archaeology and ghost research.

Finally, another entanglement that connects archaeology and ghost research is the process of **"suture"**. This is the joining together of two worlds. Archaeologist Gabriel Moshenska (2006) discusses this possible jointure when he states the following:

"The recognition of the dead as human beings like us or linked to us….as aspects of human existence is to understand them in terms of our own experiences, and thus to familiarize them" (2006:93).

Archaeology and Ghost Research: A Relational Entanglement
~ John G. Sabol ~

This speaks of human cultural entanglement, treating the "ghost", I propose, as a person, and not a measurement of space.

This book is one alternative, and hopefully, novel way of looking at relational archaeologies, and the concept of assemblages and entanglements at particular sites in ruination, ones that "haunt" us with their materializations in the present.

Photo 6: A "Traditional" Excavation (Cholula, Puebla, Mexico- 1970).

Archaeology and Ghost Research: A Relational Entanglement
~ John G. Sabol ~

Photo 7: A "Ghost Excavation"- Burnside Bridge, Antietam Battlefield, Maryland, USA- 2012).

Archaeology and Ghost Research: A Relational Entanglement
~ John G. Sabol ~

B. The "Active" Ruin that "Haunts": Transforming the Investigative Role

An archaeological site is no longer considered a "dead" world. It is rather a fluid one, imbued with vibrancy. The process of relational entanglement is a key concept. Interaction, interpretation, and meaning are based on connectivity between what remains, the performance "tools" of fieldwork, and the entanglement that emerges between contemporary acts and what remains. A ruin (or abandoned/forgotten place) is a configured site.

This configuration, I propose, is due to a multi-relational and layered stratigraphy of memory. This creates a potentially dynamic context for excavating practices. Relative entanglements are arranged in a particular way, as these specific layers of memory. These remains of the (perhaps multiple) past(s) are what materializes as spaces of possible states that "haunt". These "states" of being (or presence) become configurations of localized haunting realities, forming **"frameworks for interaction" (Latour 1996)**.

This layered entanglement of entities, spaces, memories, temporalities, and performance practices (by both the living and the dead) are the connections upon which a "ghost excavation" is based and "acted out" in the field. The "ghost excavation" is a vehicle, I propose, of relational archaeologies. This is an ex-change, a new approach in archaeological sensitivity that defines, I

Archaeology and Ghost Research: A Relational Entanglement
~ John G. Sabol ~

propose, "a process in which objects and people are made and unmade, in which they have no stable essences but are contextually and historically contingent" (Lucas 2012:166).

This relational entanglement, I propose, is dependent upon social and memory resonance. What materializes, then, is not a substance, state, or condition to be measured, as to its conformity to (or deviance from) baseline readings. These baseline readings, I propose, are not contextually relevant. This is because they don't represent (or consider) layers of ambient atmospheres (residual or interactive) tied to specific temporalities of percolating, non-sequential archaeological time.

A materialization (though present) becomes "sensed" (and recordable) when actualized, I propose, through specific social relations that entangle us with these past spatial, memory, biographical, and material configurations (or "fields"). These configurations create an "assemblage", usually in trace and fragmented form, of remains from the past that remain embedded in the present.

The role of the investigator, as "ghost excavator" at a haunting location, is not to measure and interpret deviations, scan and monitor the environment, or make demands, commanding an entity to respond in some fashion, usually via an electronic device. A role change is based on the organization of "assemblages" that materialize during performance "excavations". Through

Archaeology and Ghost Research: A Relational Entanglement
~ John G. Sabol ~

the performance of entangling (and resonating) acts, evaluation, interpretation, and understandings arise. In this process, the investigator is situated within (and becomes a part of) the "assemblage" that is now evolving during the "excavation".

The investigator is situated in a position that is located neither in the present or past, but rather actual. Through the process of relational archaeologies, a social entanglement with what (and "who") remains is becoming established. This process is shaping the haunting as an archaeological record of the traces and fragments of presence that remain from the past.

C. **Consideration and Intent: An Archaeological Orientation**

For archaeologists, the past is here and now, in this space and time (cf. Olivier 2008). As Gonzalez-Ruibal (2014) states:

"We do not have to bring the past and the present together, because they are already together. We only have to reveal their co-evalness" (2014:11).

If archaeology is about the presence of the past today, then an excavation is bringing the dead back to life. As Gonzalez-Ruibal (2014) further states:

"We make them (the dead) present and they come to speak to us. We see them....even when others do not....For archaeologists,...the past is located neither in another time, nor in another space, but *here and now*....**" (Ibid: 11).**

Ivor Noel Hume, who headed the Colonial Williamsburg Foundation's archaeological program for 30 years, has said this:

"Those who believe in the supernatural will tell you that places once the scene of great emotional or physical stress retain their energy and can release it years, even centuries, later...." (1997:146).

Archaeology and Ghost Research: A Relational Entanglement
~ John G. Sabol ~

He goes on to talk about his visit to the ruins of Green Spring in Virginia, the site of past "great emotional and physical stress":

"The trees were still; the ground was hard, cold, and crackled under foot (it was January 22, 1996)"**319 years to the day since a victorious Governor Berkeley returned.... and begin the reign of terror that so horrified the colony"**....The headlights of my parked car carried to the only still standing ruin- the one known as the jail and believed to have housed Berkeley's doomed prisoners....

Standing on the house site, I thought for a moment that I heard a women's laughter....I heard a snapping twig....Suddenly a chill blew across the open field rustling the dead grass; I pulled my coat tighter around me and was anxious to be gone. At Green Spring there should be, must be, ghosts" (Ibid: 146).

In *The Architectural Uncanny*, Anthony Vidler (1992) states that archaeology and the archaeological act (as excavation) is an uncanny act because it reveals something that was invisible. In this character, it is related to the idea of a haunting. According to Buchli and Lucas (2001), **"the idea of ghosts is very close to the archaeological imagination: the disappeared, the past, and how such spectres enthrall us, at once horrifying and comforting" (2001:12).**

Archaeology and Ghost Research: A Relational Entanglement
~ John G. Sabol ~

The archaeological act is inherently creative, **"a creative materializing intervention" (Ibid: 17).** This is what we should be doing at haunting locations, not "hunting" or measuring, and surely not waiting for something to happen by "blanketing" the space with technology!

Archaeology and Ghost Research: A Relational Entanglement
~ John G. Sabol ~

2. The Entanglement: Archaeology and Ghost Research
A. The Open Past

There are materializations that remain unexcavated. They are the remains of what may haunt us still! Archaeologist Christopher Witmore (2009) has called for an **"open past"**, and asks this: **"Is there another way to grasp entities at a distance....?" (2009:516).**

If distance means the past (as what came before), can fieldwork "excavate" what remains in ways other than what is usually practiced as archaeology? Can we do archaeology and still be **"open to the possibility that we are always dealing with realities in the plural" (Ibid: 524).**

Can we reiterate what has already been excavated? Can we re-work materials, sites, memory, and spaces to new and different ends? Can we re-entangle and interact with a past, a particular presence, a specific situation? To do this, we must first assert that there is more to be articulated!

With this in mind, let's begin our engagement, and ask ourselves the following:

- What aspects of the past can we articulate in a different way?
- How do we engage it?

Archaeology and Ghost Research: A Relational Entanglement
~ John G. Sabol ~

- What are the means to document this, one which leaves a future open for continuing articulations in ways presently unanticipated?

Archaeology and Ghost Research: A Relational Entanglement
~ John G. Sabol ~

B. Travel, Archaeology, and Those Who Remain

In order to begin (and accomplish) a journey, and that is what (in essence) ghost research is about, one has to be willing to "dig-deep". This is not a measured surface probe into the ground. It is to "dig" into questions of reality, such as this: what are we really attempting to explore at a haunted location? The reality of a truly haunting location is an exposure to new landscapes, different ways of life, values, rules, and social (sociable) engagements. We must "dig-deep", even on the surface, to experience (and record) these differences.

This *is* archaeology, and involves an archaeological sensitivity and sensibility, a means we should use to approach a perceived haunted location. This means we must de-construct our ties with the present, and re-construct a relational entanglement by socially working with what (and possibly "who") remains from what occurred in particular past events, acts, and situations in specific places and spaces.

How we approach that (those) past(s) will determine, I propose, what materializes during our "performed" excavations there. And what is the point of doing this, if we can't make it relevant in the present?

In "ghost hunting" lore, difference is assumed to be the most important phenomenon to be observed ("orbs"; shadows), recorded ("ghost box EVP), and measured (changes in EMF levels, ambient temperature). These

Archaeology and Ghost Research: A Relational Entanglement
~ John G. Sabol ~

differences call into question, according to "ghost hunting" lore, contemporary reality, making this difference (as "event") something "paranormal".

In archaeology, however, there is always the assumption of a certain degree of similarity. This is because we use analogies as useful tools (or "maps") of presence: observation in the present is analogous to what occurred in the past. This is ethnographic analogy. They must also be part of "normal", not "paranormal" reality. Ian Hodder has said that what remains these **"traces must be in some way related to social realities" (1978).**

Using sensitive and sensible excavation performance entanglements, and social analogies, in ghost research can expand our concept of contemporary reality, without considering it "paranormal". This is because we emphasize similarity (as continuity: "afterlife" existence), and not difference in what and "who" is materializing in a haunting place.

At these haunting places, one "travels" back, not remaining in present mode (contemporary behaviors, dress, and technology). By doing so, one encounters, in a deeper sense, oneself in an entanglement with something familiar, but relative to a space and time in a new, and different way (though NOT "paranormal"). This entanglement becomes **"kairotic time" (Webmoor 2013).** This occurs when time unfolds, when it percolates,

Archaeology and Ghost Research: A Relational Entanglement
~ John G. Sabol ~

as traces and fragments of the past materialize in the present.

But there remains a chord of belonging, of relating to what was just sensed. It is not something beyond our capacity to sense, or our ability to rationalize. This *is* archaeology, within the adventure and thrill of "excavation".

It is a personal connection to the people (perhaps just one individual) from the past who remain (s) at these haunting locations. After all, it is these people who should be the subjects of our study, not measured deviations or misinterpretations that become labeled as "anomalies". This also means that we must look for the similarity in any variability.

This variability is not "paranormal" in nature. It is simply a variation of a similarity: a past social entanglement through "kairotic time", and across social and spatial distance. We have a lot in common with the past, despite the assumed "barriers" between us. Our excavating entanglements give us the ability to see and sense the familiar at haunting locations. This is the key to an open mind, and an "open past".

When we explore these haunting locations, many now in a "ruined" state (or a process of ruination from what historically and socially once occurred there), we must look beyond, before the present reality. In those haunting spaces are layers of experiences and memories now entangled into a common ground today called "haunted".

Archaeology and Ghost Research: A Relational Entanglement
~ John G. Sabol ~

Even with change, there still remains the reality of stability and similarity. But we must "excavate" throughout our journey, through these (each one) layers (layer) to recover that something (someone) from the past. This becomes a growth in knowledge, a change in "latitude" and "attitude", not an anomalous event labeled "paranormal".

Archaeology and Ghost Research: A Relational Entanglement
~ John G. Sabol ~

C. The Imprint of Entanglement

We leave signature traces of our entanglements in space and time. In certain of these places, they accumulate, creating a palimpsest of haunting certainties: what came before, what continues, and what will remain in the future. This constitutes an ongoing archaeological record, a technology of memory, and what remains to haunt us with its presence. Laurent Olivier states:

"Archaeological remains are inseparable from our present....More deeply still, we are ourselves producers of archaeological materials. We do little more than add a new archaeological episode to the existence of places and things that have often already known a long series of functions and uses....We add new strata of information...." (2001:180).

That which "haunts" us with its presence is not something "paranormal", "supernatural", or "demonic". It is merely us and our ancestors. As archaeologists, we not only tell a story of the past. We also add a haunting chapter to that story of a modified space in the present-future. As Loren Eiseley (1972) says:

"Both the living and the dead revolve endlessly about an episode, a place, an event that has already been engulfed in time" (1972:229).

This is the "storied" entanglement of a haunting in the archaeological record, where past and present become the future. A haunting location, from an archaeological perspective, is a particular kind of landscape setting, a "hauntscape", where the acquisition of a particular knowledge about the past may be re-covered through performance and storytelling:

"Some landscapes….refuse history; some efface it so completely, it is never found; in others, the thronging of memories of the past subdue the living" (Loren Eiseley).

This is the entangled landscape of layers of memory. It is this "hauntscape". It is these entanglements in the landscape, as memory fields (rather than a landscape of memorials, or its re-enacted events) that we explore in relational archaeologies that I call "ghost excavations":

"knowledge is forged in the movement between places, themes, stories, and histories" (Ingold 2007:84).

This is knowledge that can be "unearthed" through the "excavation" of past entanglements at haunting locations. As an archaeologist, I "dig out" these entanglements through socially relational interactions with the "dead". In the process, I enter and become an active agent in the recovery of an expanded (not alternative or "para") history.

The remains of these social entanglements that are recovered are not complete records of past presence. They

Archaeology and Ghost Research: A Relational Entanglement
~ John G. Sabol ~

become data constructs. Fieldwork in these entangled ("haunting") locations creates a certain past from what remains, as we perform the "excavation". The record of data collection is subjective. It is based on our research goals, becoming context-dependent: what we perform to extract what remains. From these materializations of past entanglements, we construct our matrixes of haunting associations.

3. Haunting Entanglements
A. A Haunting as Entanglement

A haunted location is not the same as a site of a haunting. The former exists as "ruination", while the latter is identified as such. This is because a temporal entanglement (one or more presences of the past in the present) **"is not the source of an action but the moving target of a vast array of entities swarming toward it" (Latour 2005:46).**

A haunting location is made. They do not precede the relations that define them. These defining **"citations"** become **"attachments" (Latour 2005)** that identify a site as being haunted (through belief, appearance, perceived "anomalies", subjective experience, folklore, etc).

Archaeology and Ghost Research: A Relational Entanglement
~ John G. Sabol ~

Photo 8: A Haunting Location

Archaeology and Ghost Research: A Relational Entanglement
~ John G. Sabol ~

These "attachments" are relationships to a site that entangle together the following: place, persons, experiences, appearance, technology, and memory. The more "attachments" there are, the stronger the "haunting" entanglement becomes. These entangled associations are reinforced by repetitive behaviors, such as the continuing practices of a "ghost hunting" mindset. And these "attachments" are transferred (transmitted) to (by) others through imitation, not independent fieldwork practices.

This transfer merely translates the contemporary associated "attachment". It doesn't test past entanglements, and their re-occurrence in the present (as contextual materializations). This contemporary transfer represents contemporary continuity, not past survivorship (the "afterlife" of a particular individual or group). The result is a time-space field ("haunting" location) predisposed to reveal certain kinds of "para-histories".

But are these sites really locations of past haunting phenomenon? What is being entangled at these sites: a present to future of "living" entities (their residuals), or a past entanglement that remains present of an "afterlife, post-human entity?

Understanding this predisposition of "attachment" and relational associations is critical. Also important is a distinction between a "haunting" site and a haunted one. Analyzing the properties and qualities of past

Archaeology and Ghost Research: A Relational Entanglement
~ John G. Sabol ~

entanglements at these locations is the first step in a constructive exploration of potential <u>haunted</u> (not "haunting") locations.

We must being to understand ("leap the fence": cf. Sabol 2014) how distinct relational fields (and localized realities) might be related to social experience, both past (perhaps multiple pasts) and present. This we must do in order to build better relative (not "para") histories of these sites.

Ghost research, and its lack of legitimacy, would benefit from models that begin with some notion of relational entanglements (both present and past). We must view a potential haunted site as dynamic (not static), one that consists of social relationships that entangle not "attach" us to potentially multiple realities!

Archaeology and Ghost Research: A Relational Entanglement
~ John G. Sabol ~

Photo 9: Is This an Entangled Haunted Site?

B. The Haunting as "Actant"

A haunting is not some "thing" to measure, some "thing" that is sensed in ocular absence, some "thing" that is recorded as some "thing" anomalous. A haunting is (or can be) a vibrant matter of sociable interaction. It is not some "thing" paranormal, an estrangement from the normal, beyond reality as we perceive it. It is an entanglement, a vital materialization that can become present, <u>somebody</u> that can take shape again.

What difference would it make if a haunting was re-configured, not simply as a commodity (as it is in most "ghost hunts" and ghost tourism), but also as an **"actant" (Latour 1999)**? An "actant" is something (or someone) that can (still) do things, produce effects. In a haunting, it becomes someone whose **"competence is deduced from performance"**.

At a haunted location, I propose, this performance is social in character, an entanglement between particular people, things, space and memory. It is <u>not</u> a measurement of changing ambient conditions. Rather, it is a relation, a connection, to what occurred situationally in the past.

One must be (become) caught up in it, this entanglement. We must confront the idea of an **"open past" (Witmore 2009).** We must not think that we already know, through the laws of physics and current scientific thought, what is out there in haunted space. More so than a rational explanation, we need a relational ontology. These are

Archaeology and Ghost Research: A Relational Entanglement
~John G. Sabol ~

relational archaeologies that help us to disentangle our contemporary biases, and become attuned to the possibility of past relational entanglements that remain in contemporary space. Let's see how this entanglement can relate to what occurs in haunted space.

Archaeology and Ghost Research: A Relational Entanglement
~ John G. Sabol ~

4. The Entanglement: Haunted Sites
A. Haunted Sites: Their Temporality, Not Their "Para-History"

Tim Ingold (1993) has suggested that temporality, rather than history or chronology, emerges from the pattern of human activities in a landscape. Can we apply this concept of temporality to a haunted location, as it has been to archaeological sites?

Ingold suggests **"engaging perceptually with an environment that is itself pregnant with the past" (1993:152).** Are not haunted sites like this? Doesn't the past emerge there, leaving sensory traces that entangle together in the present?

The experience of time at haunted sites is not a history. It is simultaneous (not chronological). It is a quality of encounter that emerges (not is read) from contemporary engagements (not the narrative of past experiences). Time materializes here, but this is not a museum-like display, except for perhaps residuals of past acts. It requires, this emergence, a performance entanglement, a targeted "excavation" into a particular past entangled situation.

This temporality evokes what environmental sociologist Michael M. Bell calls a landscape as being filled with "ghosts": **"the sense of the presence of those who are not physically there" (1997:813).** But are they not? They are, I propose, if we entangle ourselves in their (not our) temporality. The place becomes a temporary space of time,

Archaeology and Ghost Research: A Relational Entanglement
~ John G. Sabol ~

what remains. It is not a site of history, or what once happened here.

A haunted site is what archaeologist Rodney Harrison (2004) calls a **"shared landscape"**. We "share" a past and engagement, not a history lesson. This is acknowledging still "living" memory, not an historian's research. It is a view of a site that is still "inhabited", not an historical catalogue of its material transformations through time:

"to inhabit the landscape is to look about, observe, (to sense), and to make sense of what one sees; it is to interpret" (Barrett 1999:26).

But one must (relationally) engage, not simply monitor or measure, to interpret. And this engagement can be multiple, defining the still "active" temporality (not history) of a layered haunted site. This temporal, and engaged, approach interacts with the past, not distances it as history and past! An excavation materializes past human lives that still inhabit the place. This is a relational process, rather than a pure description and measurement of experience and ambiance.

The temporality of haunted sites can be (are) a "mess". They are complex and a contradiction to assumed contemporary reality. This is because they are composed of multiple, sometimes conflicting, ephemeral temporal realities. Haunted sites are "still points", situations in which sensory conditions, post-human life, memory, and space are temporally-entangled and relational.

Archaeology and Ghost Research: A Relational Entanglement
~ John G. Sabol ~

Without a thorough acknowledgement and understanding of these continuing temporal entanglements, a haunting site is sensed as this "mess". It can thus be conceived as a location without rhythm or reason, something beyond the normal, thus becoming "paranormal".

But they are not. We must engage this temporality, and not describe a "para-history". We must not view this "mess" as a boundary (cf. Sabol 2014), something "set in stone". This only reinforces the concept of a haunted site as "paranormal", and not one temporally-situated within various potentially emerging and percolating relational archaeologies.

First, and foremost, these haunted sites are archaeological landscapes. They contain an embedded archaeological record of relational entanglements. We must approach this "mess" as **"permeable, contingent, and emergent, an awareness of the hybridity of archaeological landscapes... (Hicks and McAtackney 2007:25).**

Archaeology and Ghost Research: A Relational Entanglement
~ John G. Sabol ~

Photo 10: An Entangled Archaeological Landscape

B. Haunted Space

Space is a social construct. It doesn't have defined physical limits, which are socially arbitrary. If fields of energy are also unbounded (not limited to a contemporary room or structure), then their measurement is also arbitrary. A measurement of contemporary space doesn't define its temporal horizontal dimensions, or its particular vertical layers.

A haunted space is not past its time, dead and distant. It remains a living past, one that can inform the present of its presence. A relationship between the living and the not yet "dead and buried" cannot be measured by noting changes in temperature or EMF. It is achieved, I propose, through social entanglements of memory (past), performance (present), and remembrance (the haunting).

These produce memorable spaces of haunted sites. Continuity is achieved through social entanglements, a result of "excavating" performances, not a measured or monitored (and non-performing) disentanglement with what (and "who") remains from the past.

Can we define haunted space from an archaeological perspective? If we can, how? I propose that haunted space is a space where materializations associated with a particular entanglement (relative to time and social situation) occur. In order to delineate this space, we need to clearly identify the sensorial realities of those materializations. One must also distinguish between non-

Archaeology and Ghost Research: A Relational Entanglement
~ John G. Sabol ~

cultural (natural) remains and culturally-constructed, contemporary places (such as "haunting sites" in current ghost hunting lore).

The definition of haunted space begins with a manifestation that is determinable as to its entanglement in a particular past culture and time. The manifestation may occur with or without an interactive presence (a residual). It must be part of a set of relationships (relational archaeologies) between:

- What happened there in that space in the past;
- Contain a trace or fragment that could remain from a past event, situation, or act; and
- Resonate with the entanglement created by the investigator during a "performance excavation".

If we re-create these social entanglements in haunted space, combining things, experience, people, and memory, we become encultured and emplaced in that space. We become part of the entanglement of that which "haunts" that space.

These relational entanglements in haunted space between what remains of the past, and the "excavating" performances of contemporary investigators, are a rite of passage (Van Gennep 1960). It is a form of emplacement positioning in a space that is haunted by past presence:

- It is a position of separation from the present;

Archaeology and Ghost Research: A Relational Entanglement
~ John G. Sabol ~

- It is entering a position of liminality between a present and past that becomes a means to create a social entanglement; and
- It becomes a position of re-incorporation, the entanglement with the past that remains.

Through this process of entanglement in a haunted space, we become bound to a particular layer of past social interaction. We entangle ourselves within the haunting, and not arbitrarily measuring some (possibly) unbounded residual field; or waiting for a spontaneous manifestation to occur, itself unbounded by context, association, and specific-defining meaning.

Using a relational and entangled process in a potentially haunted space means the development of a different strategy of investigative fieldwork. This includes:

- The determination of cultural coordinates (the social strata of occupation) and positioning (what performance roles and what situation);
- The determination of temporality (what time frame); and
- The determination of materiality and sensoriality (what targeting tools ("triggers") do we use.

Today in ghost research, there is a fixation, from "ghost tech" to a haunting itself, with "things" as some "thing" to be measured, recorded, and displayed on social media. Ghost hunting and "paranormal investigations" have

Archaeology and Ghost Research: A Relational Entanglement
~ John G. Sabol ~

evolved to an involvement (an entanglement) with the consumption of material culture in perceived haunted spaces. This has led to a significant influence on the social construction and negotiation of a particular identity (and entity) labeled "ghost hunter" or "paranormal investigator", both non-relational beings in <u>any</u> haunted space!

Where does this lead us to a broader understanding of past social dynamics with entities that haunt? By focusing on the process of materialization, rather than "discovery" (the "ghost in the machine" as measured and recorded), our entangled field performances in haunted space can facilitate a more critical disciplinary approach to a haunting. It can also allow for a more pronounced social (not "paranormal") purpose.

Today, we still have not withdrawn from outside the spaces (and places) that constitute a perceived haunted location. We live with these "ghosts". We are entangled among them. But we must understand that entanglement. As archaeologist Laurent Olivier states:

"In fact, neither places nor things say anything whatsoever in themselves, unless it is to those who have memories of them" (2001:184).

We must re-connect with those memories, become entangled in what happened there in haunted space. We must, through these entanglements, tell their stories. We don't do this by inventing (without considerable

Archaeology and Ghost Research: A Relational Entanglement
~ John G. Sabol ~

justification and verification) a "para-history" of these haunted spaces!

This doing something must be relational and contextual to what happened there because what remains (to be worked with) will be those memories and experiences that occurred there. They are not something new or different (such as "make the light blink on that electronic device").

This is because "traces" and "fragments" of past remains must be in some way related to social realities, as archaeologist Ian Hodder has stated. Fieldwork in haunted space is, I propose, an "excavation" of relational archaeologies. They are not the measurement of a "paranormal" event.

If archaeology is **"the systematic recording of material traces....or simply as 'digging beneath the surface of things'" (Hodder 2001:190)**, then archaeological acts are positioned as a good baseline for archaeological-type methods in haunted space. If a haunting is someone (whether a residual element or an interactive presence) that persists in haunted space, and archaeology **"involves the idea of excavating to layers below the verbal, conscious, represented" (Ibid: 191),** then ghost research in haunted space is within the scope of a relational archaeology.

The "excavation" of this haunted space is part of the "archaeological imagination". Shanks (2012) identifies components of this archaeological imagination (2012:146-

Archaeology and Ghost Research: A Relational Entanglement
~ John G. Sabol ~

148), many of which could apply to the investigation of haunted space. These include:

- "performative paradigms of engagement with the remains of the past";
- "an uncanny sense of a haunting past";
- "ruin and phantasm: bits remaining of the past as well as traces....and imprints";
- "uncanningly non-absent phantasms, hauntingly present"; and
- "modeling worlds on the basis of fragments".

Ghost research requires particular performances that entangle the investigator with what happened in the past. Relational archaeologies (as "performance excavations"), I propose, are those means to connect with what (and "who") remains of past entanglements in a haunted space.

Performance is a creative process which can make manifest the past. These materializations become a cultural model of remaining past presence. This model is based on social entanglement, and this is not a "paranormal event". Rather, it is an exercise in the use of the archaeological imagination in particular spaces deemed "haunted".

Archaeology and Ghost Research: A Relational Entanglement
~ John G. Sabol ~

C. The "Host" and the "Ghosts"

In haunted space, it's "Welcome to our World", not a welcome to our contemporary one. That's where "ghost hunters" (and "paranormal investigators") get it wrong! This is because the haunted site is the "host" that which is <u>at</u> site (what remains of past presences there). It's the "host" that has (maintains) **"personality, history, character, narrative** (and memory) **written into it" (McLucas, quoted in Morgan 1995:47).**

If we change or alter this entanglement, we become something (somebody) else. This is:

"to construct another architecture within the existing architecture (and entanglement)**, imposing another arrangement, floor plan, map, or orientation which confounds everyday hierarchies of place and patterns of movement" (Pearson 2007).**

Isn't this what ghost hunters do, with their tech devices that measure contemporary ambient space and architectural features? And isn't this what a "command and demand" stance ("Can you……; "Do something!") does to past social entanglements and former relational situations?

This is a cultural mismatch, not a social relation between "host" and who comes after the events of the past! This creates tension and confusion **"through the employment of orders of material seemingly unusual,**

Archaeology and Ghost Research: A Relational Entanglement
~ John G. Sabol ~

inappropriate or perverse at this site" (Pearson 2010:36). The "host" (the site) and its "ghosts" experience the "ghost" (the contemporary "ghost hunter")! This creates potential confrontation ("get out") because of ignorance, unreconciled non-relational entanglements between place, space, people, memory, and material culture.

"Ghost hunting" creates "ghosts": themselves! Their entertaining performances are active agents for most (if not all) non-materializations. This is because they ignore (for whatever reasons) the fact that the haunted site is still (for relational archaeologies) an active agent, **"either formally (in architectural or spatial terms) or socially and culturally (in political ownership or historical terms)" (McLucas 1993:6).**

The problem is "ghost hunters" have not disentangled themselves from the present and its technology, and re-assembled their reality to conform to the relationalities of the past (perhaps multiple pasts) at haunted sites. They do not know how to properly socially-engage what remains of the past!

In a "ghost excavation", we respect and honor the "host" conditions. We do this through relational archaeologies that entangle us with past presences (see Sabol 2014). In this resonating role, we become witnesses to what and "who" remains. A "ghost excavation" and haunting materializations constitute, I propose, a temporary, unique

Archaeology and Ghost Research: A Relational Entanglement
~ John G. Sabol ~

relational entanglement between "host" and witness (or witnesses) that is not technology-driven.

These entanglements create cultural production at a haunted location. It is creative work that maps continuing practices and behaviors. As the "excavators" of these entanglements, we are ourselves part of the process of emergent materialization, witnesses to it (and not the "ghosts" within it).

This entanglement is a gathering of associations in a "gathered" place (a "host" space), in which boundaries are crossed (see Sabol 2014): the past and the present; and the living and the dead. The entanglements of relational fields become materializing entanglements of experiences between host and witness, not host and ghost.

The interaction of these sensually-related fields creates a haunting, not haunted space. This is because this is a creative, not measured, process. It is the making of materialization through relational archaeologies. It is not a vigil or a monitoring of space, waiting for it (a manifestation) to occur.

In a haunted location, as the "host" site, the materializations are ephemeral, dynamic, becoming, and disconnecting. It is an entanglement in constant flux as an "open past". It is not simply a measured line connecting past to present, absence to presence, or the dead to the living. It is a pathway, opened momentarily, to a series of social connections, relationships, and memories.

Archaeology and Ghost Research: A Relational Entanglement
~ John G. Sabol ~

These entanglements at host (haunted) sites are fields of convergence that absorb resonance and re-arrange realities. They have the capacity to transform particular spaces and places, and with that, the experiences of individuals within the field of entanglement.

Any one host site is potentially an engagement with multiple, entangled layers of memory and presence. That's why, to engage each, we must know what the past entanglements contained, and how to connect and interact with them. Otherwise, it is us who will be (and remain) the "ghost"!

Archaeology and Ghost Research: A Relational Entanglement
~ John G. Sabol ~

Photo 11: Is this Residual the "Host" or the "Ghost"?: Burnside Bridge, Antietam Battlefield (Maryland)

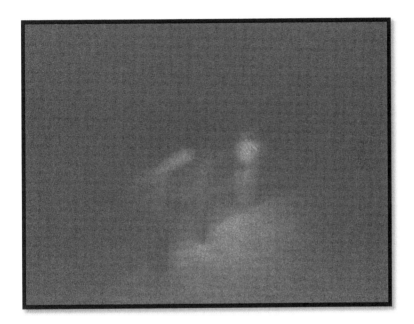

Archaeology and Ghost Research: A Relational Entanglement
~ John G. Sabol ~

5. Excavating the Entanglement

A. The Entangled Archaeological "Ghost Culture"

In a relational entanglement at a haunted site, we extend cultural agency (intentional acts) to materializations in spaces perceived to be inhabited by "spirits" or "ghosts". Contemporary people and these animate entities would both be the creators of acts (social behaviors) and "cultures" (as each site entanglement would be socially different).

This "ghost culture" is composed of, I propose, a series of fragmented "assemblages", or a series of "assembling" relations. This constitutes the "afterlife" world of trans-humans who continue in a physical entanglement with other humans, spaces, and fields of memory.

This is taking seriously a haunted site ontology, the cultural entanglement that maintains a place as "haunted". Human practices today, and the embedded memories of past acts, involve social relations that are entangled. And the traces of these interactions exist and can be documented.

And these entanglements to (with) what occurred in the past is a significant part of exploring and "excavating" places that are embedded with layers of remains that exhibit particular spatial and temporal characteristics. Nancy Munn (1992) asserts:

Archaeology and Ghost Research: A Relational Entanglement
~ John G. Sabol ~

"In a lived world, spatial and temporal dimensions cannot be disentangled, and the two comingle in various ways" (1992:94).

One place in which they comingle, I propose, is a haunted site. And a haunting becoming materialized, represents entangled traces and fragments of particular layers of past events, acts, and situations in specific spaces and temporalities at these sites. These are archaeological space/time dimensions. Each represents a particular archaeological "ghost culture".

At haunted locations, what survives is a fragmented biography, or (in some cases: a battlefield) traces of **"communities of memory" (Burke 1989)**. They remain embedded through memories of acts and interactions that bind individuals, groups, and a sensory culture (an entangled "ghost culture") together, over and through time. In this process of entanglement, they create a haunted sense of relational archaeologies.

In my "ghost excavations", I attempt to "unearth" the memories of these entanglements, as a post-human "ghost culture", through performing in these past entanglements. This includes auditory cues (temporally-identified "soundmarks"), associations with objects (as "triggers"), and the repetition of situations that perpetuate a sense of relational entanglement (see Rappaport 1990).

This entangled combination of sight, sound, (and perhaps smell) provides an "excavation" framework of temporality.

Archaeology and Ghost Research: A Relational Entanglement
~ John G. Sabol ~

It produces a particular energetic rhythm from which materializations can potentially emerge. At a haunted location, this entanglement plays a central role in shaping and facilitating the recall of something (and someone) absent.

Photo 12: A "Ghost Excavation"

Archaeology and Ghost Research: A Relational Entanglement
~ John G. Sabol ~

This entanglement of past remains (the "ghost culture") is "excavated" through a process that connects memory to intervention (performance practices): what we could affect, and what affects us. At the 2014 T.A.G. (Theoretical Archaeology Group) conference at the University of Illinois (Urbana-Champagne), archaeologist Kenneth E. Sassaman (University of Florida) identifies this as a four step process:

- **"sensualize the past";**
- **"socialize the sensual";**
- **"emplace the social";** and
- **"network the places".**

Our work at the Daniel Lady farm near Gettysburg, Pennsylvania is an example of the application of this four step process of entanglement:

- We "sensualized the past" by embedding ourselves in what occurred at that farm in the aftermath of the battle of Gettysburg;
- We "socialized" this by performing different social roles at the farm, all contextual to what had occurred there in July 1863;
- We "emplaced" these social roles in various scenarios relative to caring for the wounded soldiers, and conducting simulated amputations; and

Archaeology and Ghost Research: A Relational Entanglement
~ John G. Sabol ~

- We "networked" these scenarios at various places on the farm: in the barn where the amputations occurred; in the house with the trauma endured by the family; and outside the barn where bodies were located by cadaver dogs.

Archaeology and Ghost Research: A Relational Entanglement
~ John G. Sabol ~

Photo 13: The "Excavation" of the Daniel Lady Farm (Gettysburg, Pennsylvania)

Archaeology and Ghost Research: A Relational Entanglement
~ John G. Sabol ~

Photo 14: Daniel Lady Farm "Excavation"

Archaeology and Ghost Research: A Relational Entanglement
~ John G. Sabol ~

Photo 15: Daniel Lady Farm "Excavation"

Archaeology and Ghost Research: A Relational Entanglement
~ John G. Sabol ~

Each "ghost excavation" is different, not just in belief systems, but also in their relational archaeological practices: sociability, participants, memories, spaces embedded, and experiences. This affects the nature and character of the potential materializations. The past world(s) of haunted space is, thus, configured (entangled) differently, so the types and degree of what is haunting can differ from site to site. This means that there are different relational ontologies, and different localized realities of this "ghost culture" that remain at haunted locations.

Exploring and participating in these remaining localized realities (particular "ghost cultures") gives us new present realities as various entanglements merge. This produces materializing presents becoming manifest out of these past localized realities. And we record that past as we involve ourselves in those past entanglements. Thus, what becomes present (the "ghost culture") are ongoing participatory flows that are inseparable from the contemporary performed entanglements directed ("targeted") at those in the past.

Archaeology and Ghost Research: A Relational Entanglement
~ John G. Sabol ~

B. <u>Relational Archaeologies and the Haunted Site</u>

A haunted site is a potentially complex setting where the remains of past presence are embedded. It is not merely a "haunted house", building, or landscape. It certainly is not a haunted "hallowed ground". It was (and remains) an entanglement between place, objects, spaces, time, and ritualistic/habitual behaviors. All of these elements of entanglement are part of archaeological fieldwork. Thus, a haunted site should represent a relational archaeology of place, and explored as a series of connections of relational archaeologies.

Place, as an archaeological entity, can have many representations through time, portraying different meanings to different people. Similarly, a haunted site is a place with many meanings, both past and contemporary. These various entanglements within the spaces of a place serve these different functions, relative to agency, social behavior, and occupational history (as events and situations; habitual acts).

But the extent of place in archaeological terms is limited by excavation (vertically) and survey (horizontally). Fieldwork is an arbitrary practice defined by funding, research scope, and stratigraphy. But can place, as haunted space, be extended beyond the physical dimensions of "digging"?

Can an event, a dramatic situation, a performance, even habitual acts, continue to constitute place? Can multiple

Archaeology and Ghost Research: A Relational Entanglement
~ John G. Sabol ~

manifestations of these remains, as a particular stratum of entangled memories, be perceived and recorded today in certain places?

The exploration of these types of places, using an archaeological approach, would not be limited by physical excavations. It would be expanded through "performance excavations", using particular entanglements ("triggers" as tools of excavation) that would aid in the "unearthing" of what remains of each past entangled occupation.

These "triggers' (contextual cultural scenarios) serve as "actants'. And the entanglement of contemporary excavation would revolve around two entities:

- The place: this is the connection that draws different remains together; and
- The haunting entanglement: these are the stories, the different past performances that remain in place (embedded) in the site.

Cultural behaviors ritualize a site. Their performance acts define a life, separating areas of activity, outlining identity, and establishing a series of spaces within a place. This entangles a presence (ritually or habitually) to a certain mode of being. This certain mode is what remains, and manifests as a haunting. As remains are embedded in a strata of ground in a physical excavation, so too these haunting remains are embedded in an entanglement of memories, behaviors, rituals, and habitual routines.

Archaeology and Ghost Research: A Relational Entanglement
~ John G. Sabol ~

To disengage these remains from their embedded context, we must re-entangle ourselves into that particular embedded context. This is fieldwork as a "performance excavation", or what I call a "ghost excavation".

Archaeology is an exploration of material culture. Can a "ghost excavation" unearth the remains of a material (or sensory) "ghost culture" that defines a haunted place? In a "ghost excavation", place (as haunted) becomes an "assemblage" that is associated with various past social entanglements.

These entanglements remain as "fractures": traces, vestiges, and residuals from the past. It is these remains that we must document in context: relative to a particular past entanglement that is recorded in an ethno-historical narrative (relational archaeologies).

How do we "unearth" a past entangled (and embedded) trace, vestige, or residual? We do this by creating a similar entanglement in the present. To do this, we have to think of time at a haunted location as circular, not linear. Time there is not a dead, buried, and distanced history (past).

In a "ghost excavation", we are, therefore, not re-enacting a past. Time is the past continuing into, being entangled with, and informing the present (actuality). In a "ghost excavation", we are creating an entanglement to connect with a "live" contemporary past.

Archaeology and Ghost Research: A Relational Entanglement
~ John G. Sabol ~

Photo 16: A "Ghost Excavation"

Archaeology and Ghost Research: A Relational Entanglement
~ John G. Sabol ~

We reinforce that contemporary past social entanglement through the manipulation of memories, as material (objects and clothing) and sensory (sounds and smells) "triggers". This is a form of object animation. We use "things" (objects) to re-animate the presences that may remain embedded at the location.

These "animating" objects do have agency. But they don't "haunt" us. They "haunt" those who remain. These objects are a **"technology of memory" (Thomas 1993)**, or **"technologies of remembrance" (Johnson & Sneider 2013)**. Being relative to a past entanglement, they can also be thought of as forms of a past identification of time, since **"objects anchor time" (Tuan 1977:123)**.

What we are attempting to do in a "ghost excavation", through our performance practices, is the generation of a ritual time (see Bloch 1971), a re-cycled time through relational archaeologies of entanglements.

At a haunted location, much of this past entanglement can be sensed as various forms of sensory elements. These sensorial experiences of a haunted location (or any place that has been defined as a "heterotopy" (Balissac 2013)). This sense of place equates well with archaeology of place:

"lived bodily experience of a place and landscape (is) a continuous process of sensorial interactions. The body is both enculturated and emplaced" (Tilley 1999:180).

Archaeology and Ghost Research: A Relational Entanglement
~ John G. Sabol ~

This is the entanglement, I propose, we experience in a "ghost excavation" with a haunting contemporary past. This emplacement can result from the entanglement between the experience of relational and contextual performances, and the materiality (what remains) of past place entanglements (see also de Nardi 2013).

In a "ghost excavation", our performance practices, as relational enactments with our bodies, is one form of "measuring" space and place. As Gheorghiu and Nash (2013) suggest:

"one can say the 'human being is the measure of all places'" (2013:9).

This "measurement" is a "geo-metry", **"which is the science of the relationships between parts" (Ibid: 9).** It is the entanglement that we seek in a "ghost excavation". Is this entanglement a natural one, one with embedded past entities? I propose that it is. And this has archaeological precedence. Lucero (2008) states that archaeological work among the Maya **"reflect that houses were not just homes, but charged places embodying the living and the dead (2008:204).**

Archaeology and Ghost Research: A Relational Entanglement
~John G. Sabol ~

C. <u>Animating a Haunted Site</u>

Relational archaeologies are based on open-ended conceptualizations of particular past realities. Simply put, not all hauntings or haunted locations are the same. We cannot go into a "general" ghost hunt mode (survey; measure; demand/command; monitor) at all sites, or use an arsenal of still unproven methods, technologies, and practices. Thinking a "ghost" is just a "ghost", and a "haunting" is just a "haunting" does not advance the field!

Fieldwork practices ought to be unique singularities that emerge from research with ethno-historical data and contexts, rather than general frameworks and "copied" formulas of investigative execution that are applied to all cases of a suspected haunting.

The false assumption that there are no experts only leads to a literal "free for all": anyone can do this fieldwork (even children), and any method can be used. That's why "ghost hunting" is a "mess"! It's why ghost research doesn't get recognition as a legitimate field of inquiry. This "mindset" will result in non-predictable manifesting expectations, a result of materially-different past entanglements emerging.

This creates the appearance of an "anomaly", something beyond what is normally expected or predicted. This does not make that manifestation a paranormal event. It merely shows the lack of control (and context) of a typical "ghost hunt". Such anomalies reinforce the formulation of "ghost

Archaeology and Ghost Research: A Relational Entanglement
~ John G. Sabol ~

hunting" categories of a haunting, concepts of how to do fieldwork, and definitions of what should be done (and "ghost hunt" relevant) and what is not. This hinders a goal of producing new concepts (cf. Henare, et.al. 2007), or expanding our existing categories of thought (Viveros de Castro 2006).

To advance the field, we must break the bond of dualist structures (past/present; absence/presence; normal/paranormal; dead/alive). This alternative stance does not sacrifice scientific thinking. It reaches for a means to articulate the complexity (and variety) of haunting phenomena.

To say that both people (investigators) and "ghosts" require "social" work to initiate (and maintain) a relational entanglement, is to suggest a commonality between the two, and not a difference (the dualist structure). To incorporate this relational concept into fieldwork is to change the terms of the use, execution, and display of concepts, definitions, and data in ghost research.

This becomes not a "hunt" in (for) a past, but rather an intervention, a work in progress in the present. It is about how a past presence can become present. And this is not a new world revealed as a "para-history", but rather an older one (perhaps multiple older ones) recovered through a "para-ontology"!

6. Summary
A. The Contemporary and Future Relevance and Relation of a "Ghost Excavation"

Archaeology today is about more than ruins, decay, or simply surveys and excavations. It is also about authenticity, "afterlives", heritage, disaster, and presence in absence (among many others). They are unfolding still to be relational potentialities for an archaeology of the contemporary past. The continuing reality of the past in the present is still unfolding in an open past. Some of these archaeologies represent a sometimes unauthorized trespass into (and onto) the lives and "afterlives" of contemporary and past peoples.

Archaeology is not the study <u>of</u> the past, but a study <u>with</u> it: **"archaeology studies with the remains of the past which have endured in some form into the present" (Fowler 2013:4).** If a haunting exists, and there are ghosts of the past, then a ghost that haunts is one form the past exists in the present.

And if **"we engage with the remains of the past in order to consider something other than those remains" (Ibid: 4)**, then ghost research, as an archaeological endeavor, is about what a haunting tells us about continuity, not "life after death". This is an attempt to explore the entanglements that composed and transformed the remains of past bodies and places.

Archaeology and Ghost Research: A Relational Entanglement
~ John G. Sabol ~

There is also the paradox between a present archaeological gaze of landscape and its material remains, and the archaeological work that is required to generate knowledge about "what remains". What still lies hidden from the present is vast. And in that exploration of the archaeological record, we are both close to and distant from that which we study.

Fieldwork at haunted locations becomes a re-orientation of (and toward) archaeological practices. It is a concern for both the living and the dead, and the entanglement of the past, the present, and the future within the field of inquiry. Investigations in haunted space become a creative, performance process. It involves assembling contemporary and historical material, in spaces where they intervene in the present, in relational archaeologies.

In my fieldwork, I am especially interested in the process of assemblage at these locations that are considered haunted. This foregoes the appropriation of the past, creatively re-imagined in the present, as a "paranormal" event.

In a "ghost excavation", there is a concern with the "afterlife" of what remains from a past that is still percolating in the present. There is a focus on how we can connect with it through these relational archaeologies. This is social interaction that is made, not given (or expected).

A performance "excavation" becomes a specific archaeological mediation of time, connecting to spectral

Archaeology and Ghost Research: A Relational Entanglement
~ John G. Sabol ~

traces (simultaneously past and present; absent and emerging). This re-mediation creates a future emergence. It becomes the simultaneous time of the past and the future in the present, something we have experienced many times during a "ghost excavation".

These relational archaeologies come to involve themselves not only with contemporary sensory materializations of past reality, but also potential futures which are embodied and evoked through these relational entanglements. It is an archaeology that reminds us how to "salvage" these emerging remains as forms of **"exorcising the past" (cf. Harrison and Schofield 2010).** This is imagining a future in which this lost or neglected past (as a "fringe" study) continues to be significant in the present-future.

B. The Cardinal Rule: What/"Who" Remains Is "Heritage"

All haunted sites, be they archaeological ruins or historical places in disuse, are "hallowed grounds". They are places that have left an imprint, a residual presence that says "this happened here!" They should be treated as sites of socio-cultural human heritage. What and "who" remains must be preserved with a concept of heritage in mind.

Photo 17: A "Haunted Heritage Site

Archaeology and Ghost Research: A Relational Entanglement
~ John G. Sabol ~

As Charles Pellegrino states in *Ghosts of Vesuvius* (2005):

"I do know that I was always careful never to pollute the Titanic, or any archaeological site, with objects from my own time. Injunctions against such contamination (to avoid confusing archaeologists of the future) were always a cardinal rule in the field...." (2005:389).

So too with haunted locations, as both these and other archaeological sites are heritage sites (not sites of contemporary entertainment). We must not contaminate the haunted site with contemporary technologies, as these are potentially still (at least some of them) "living" sites.

Relational archaeologies, a mix of people, things, memory, beliefs, and acts are part of entangled strata of presence. Introducing "foreign" elements destroys this relational symmetry and negates the important concept of layered context, so necessary in archaeology <u>and</u> ghost research.

This heritage that is a haunted site is no "ghost" of the imagination, certainly not the archaeological imagination. It is not a measured contemporary environmental deviation or reading. It is not a "beep" or a "blinking light" on an electronic device used in "ghost hunting".

These contemporary manifestations were not part of the original social entanglements in past spaces. So their manifestations today (whatever they are or mean) are part of a newly-entangled contemporary space and context.

Archaeology and Ghost Research: A Relational Entanglement
~ John G. Sabol ~

The past in the present does not mean the present in the past!

Archaeology and Ghost Research: A Relational Entanglement
~ John G. Sabol ~

Photo 18: Another Haunted Heritage Site

Archaeology and Ghost Research: A Relational Entanglement
~John G. Sabol ~

Appendix

Haunted Houses as Relational Archaeologies

"Wherever there is an entity with multiple states, there is some consciousness. You need a special structure to get a lot of it, but consciousness is everywhere….".

- **Giulio Tononi, Neuroscientist**

A haunting is a particular **"structure of feeling" (Williams 1977)**, and a "house" as "home" is an entity with possible multiple states (depending upon the number of occupancies in its history). If "consciousness is everywhere", as Tononi states, then it "haunts" all our residences we call "home".

This means that one particular dwelling does not enclose it (consciousness). We can create a new "consciousness" of home as we move, yet still retain a "residual" (as something experienced, perhaps differently) in previous places we once lived. We can potentially "haunt" multiple sites, even without being "dead"! Add to this, the continued residences of a house by others, both living and in the past, and we have a varied stratigraphy of memories that become attached to these structures.

A house (or any structure) can become a potent mix of potential energy, both residual and interactive, past and present, all entangled in a place once (and sometimes still)

Archaeology and Ghost Research: A Relational Entanglement
~ John G. Sabol ~

called "home". This "haunting" can perhaps consist of a large assemblage of social actors and their performances. The re-use of a building, a home, a structure (even a landscape) creates a palimpsest of entanglements that become embedded onto the spaces of these sites.

A surface "hunt" that attempts to document these presences cannot penetrate through the entangled layers, nor can it distinguish between one embedded context and that of another. What it does, by not being relational to what previously occurred there, is to create another (additional) layer of entanglement. And a subsequent "ghost hunt", using the same methods, can sustain this form of <u>contemporary</u> haunting!

A place perceived to be haunted can create subsequent intentionality. Once the memory of a haunting experience is mediated, it controls future practices there by channeling subsequent acts and feelings. The "haunted" site becomes a landscape in memory. The continuing "ghost hunting" practices maintain its haunted nature, and how these places, in turn, recreate this haunting and the memory of it.

This entanglement between humans ("ghost hunters"), their practices ("ghost hunting"), and space (a perceived haunted location) show how non-human things (the site) cause others (contemporary humans) to act in a certain way. While the location may or may not be haunted, and there may or may not be "ghosts" there with intentions to

Archaeology and Ghost Research: A Relational Entanglement
~ John G. Sabol ~

communicate, it (the entanglement) can cause practices to happen, and become embedded as haunting memories.

This is the way that a memory of a haunting begins and is maintained, forming part of the continuing entanglement through time. It is creating memories, and passing them on, from this entanglement of chains of "ghost hunting" repetitions.

How do we investigate this, explore a site's enormous potential? Do we "hunt" for answers? Do we measure environmental conditions? Do we "debunk" the experiences of others?

In this relationality that is a structure, relative to potentially multiple (and perhaps different) entanglements, what does one "hunt": people, things, experiences, memories? Is the "hunt" about something (someone) past or present? What is one measuring: a past residual or a contemporary one; an interactive past or a contemporary "anomaly"?

If one measures, what are the entanglements of that (those) measurements? How do you "debunk", distinguishing past from present, natural from social? The list goes on. Are all these entangled energies different frequencies operating in a "home" that is currently occupied? Is the entanglement the same measurement in a visibly abandoned structure?

How does one disentangle the entanglements between past/present, absence/presence, dead/alive, and

Archaeology and Ghost Research: A Relational Entanglement
~ John G. Sabol ~

residual/interactive? If everything that happened in a house or structure is potentially still there, how do you investigate this? If the concept of time does not apply to consciousness, how do you separate the layers of consciousness, experiences, and memories as materializing presences?

To do this, we must disengage ourselves from the present, and re-engage that potential layer(s) of the past that remain embedded. We do this by re-connecting to those (each layer independently) past entanglements. These are relational archaeologies that deal with the potentially multiple layers of a haunting that entangle these sites.

We do an "excavation" to disentangle ourselves from the present. This is an intervention, but a non-intrusive one. The key word is "affect": how our intervention affects those who remain. We don't want to alter past entanglements. We want to immerse ourselves in them. We do this by "excavating" relational performances.

In "excavating" or surveying a haunted (or a potentially haunted) site, it is essential to explore the full "historiography" or memory of (in) the site, both past and present. It is part of understanding how humans construct and maintain identity and social practices, perhaps even some as an "afterlife" performance.

Archaeology and Ghost Research: A Relational Entanglement
~ John G. Sabol ~

Photo 19: What are the layers of Entanglement Here?

Bibliography

Ackroyd, Peter. 2010. *The English Ghost: Spectres Through Time.* London: Vintage

Alberti, Benjamin. 2013. *Archaeology and Ontologies of Scale: The Case of Miniaturization in First-Millennium Northwest Argentina* in *Archaeology After Interpretation: Returning Materials to Archaeological Theory.* Benjamin Alberti, Andrew M. Jones, and Joshua Pollard (Editors). Walnut Creek, California: Left Coast Press, Inc. pp. 43-58.

Balissac, Paul. 2013. *Space and Time as Cultural Artifact: Blackpool as Heterotopy.* in *Archaeology After Interpretation.* Benjamin Alberti, Andrew M. Jones, and Joshua Pollard (Editors). Walnut Creek, California: Left Coast press, Inc. pp. 55-64.

Barrett, J.C. 1999. *Chronologies of Landscape* in P. Ucko and R. Layton (Editors) *The Archaeology and Anthropology of Landscape.* London: Routledge. pp. 21-30.

Bell, Michael M. 1997. *The Ghosts of Place.* Theory and Society 26: 813-836.

Bennett, J. 2010. *Vibrant Matter.* Durham, North Carolina: Duke University Press.

Bloch, M. 1971. *The Past and the Present in the Present.* Man 12: 278-92.

Archaeology and Ghost Research: A Relational Entanglement
~ John G. Sabol ~

Buchli, V. and Gavin Lucas 2001. *The Absent Present: Archaeology of the Contemporary Past* in *Archaeologies of the Contemporary Past*. V. Buchli and Gavin Lucas (Editors). London: Routledge. pp. 3-18.

Burke, Peter. 1989. *History as Social Memory* in *Memory, History, Culture, and the Mind*. Edited by Thomas Butler. Oxford: Basil Blackwell. Pp. 97-113.

DeNardi, Sarah. 2013. *How Natural are Natural Places? Challenging Stereotypes in the Interpretation of Landscape in Iron Age Veneto, Italy* in *Archaeology After Interpretation*. Benjamin Alberti, Andrew M. Jones, and Joshua Pollard (Editors). Walnut Creek, California: Left Coast Press, Inc. pp.277-298.

Dreyfus, Hubert L. and Paul Rabinow. 1983. *Michel Foucault: Beyond Structuralism and Hermeneutics*. Chicago: University of Chicago Press.

Eiseley, Loren. 1972. *The Night Country*. New York: Charles Scribner's Sons.

Emerson T.E., and T.R. Pauketat (Editors). 1997. *Cahokia: Domination and Ideology in the Mississippian*. Lincoln: University of Nebraska Press.

Fowler, Chris. 2013. *The Emergent Past: A Relational Realist Archaeology of Early Bronze Age Mortuary Practices*. Oxford: Oxford University Press.

Geertz, Clifford. 1973. *The Interpretation of Cultures.* New York: Basic Books.

Geiger, Clarence R. and Stephen R. Potter. 2003. *Archaeological Perspectives on the American Civil War.* Gainesville: University Press of Florida.

Gheorghiu, D. and George Nash. 2013. *Place, Materiality, Time, and Ritual: Towards a Relational Archaeology* in *Archaeology After Interpretation.* Benjamin Alberti, Andrew M. Jones, and Joshua Pollard (Editors). Walnut Creek, California: Left Coast Press, Inc. pp. 1-12.

Gonzalez-Ruibal, Alfredo. 2013. *Reclaiming Archaeology* in *Reclaiming Archaeology: Beyond the Tropes of Modernity.* Alfredo Gonzalez-Ruibal (Editor). London: Routledge. pp. 1-30.

2014. *Returning to Where We Have Never Been: Excavating the Ruins of Modernity* in *Ruin Memories: Materialities, Aesthetics, and the Archaeology of the Recent Past.* Bjornar Olsen and Dora Petursdottir (Editors). London: Routledge. pp. 367-389.

Gordillo, Gaston. 2009. *Places that Frighten: Residues of Wealth and Violence on the Argentine Chaco Frontier. Anthropogica* 51: *343-351.*

Graves-Brown, Paul, Rodney Harrison, and Angela Piccini. 2013. *Introduction* in *The Oxford Handbook of the Archaeology of the Contemporary World.* Oxford: Oxford University Press.

Archaeology and Ghost Research: A Relational Entanglement
~ John G. Sabol ~

Harrison, Rodney. 2004. *Shared Landscapes: Archaeologies of Attachment and the Pastoral Industry in New South Wales.* Sydney: New South Wales Press.

2011. *Surface Assemblages: Toward an Archaeology in and of the present.* Archaeological Dialogues 18(2):141-96.

Harrison, Rodney and John Schofield. 2010. *After Modernity: Archaeological Approaches to the Contemporary Past.* Oxford: Oxford University Press.

Henare, A. 2007. *Introduction: Thinking Through Things* in *Thinking Through Things: Theorizing Artifacts Ethnographically.* M. Holbraad and S. Wastell (Editors). London: Routledge. pp. 1-31.

Hicks, Dan and Laura McAtackney. 2007. *Introduction: Landscapes as Standpoints* in *Envisioning Landscapes, Situations, and Standpoints in Archaeology and Heritage.* D. Hicks, L. McAtackney, and G. Fairclough (Editors). Walnut Creek, California: Left Coast Press, Inc. pp.13-29.

Hodder, Ian. 1978. *Always Momentary, Fluid, and Flexible: Towards a Reflexive Excavation Methodology. Antiquity* 71: 691-700.

2001. *Epilogue* in *Archaeologies of the Contemporary Past.* V. Buchli and Gavin Lucas (Editors). London: Routledge pp. 189-191.

2012. *Entangled: An Archaeology of the Relationships Between Humans and Things.* Oxford, U.K.: Wiley-Blackwell.

Archaeology and Ghost Research: A Relational Entanglement
~ John G. Sabol ~

Holtorf, Cornelius. 2008. *Notes on the Life History of a Pot Sherd* in *Reading Archaeology: An Introduction.* Edited by Robert J. Muckle. Peterborough, Ontario, Canada: Broadview Press. pp. 156-169.

Hume, Ivor Noel. 1997. *In Search of This and That: Tales From an Archaeologist's Quest.* Williamsburg, Virginia: The Colonial Williamsburg Foundation.

Ingold, Tim. 1993. *The Temporality of Landscape. World Archaeology* 25(2): 152-174.

2007. *Materials Against Materiality. Archaeological Dialogues* 14(1): 1-16.

Johnson, James A. and Seth A. Sneider. 2013. *Materiality of Place, Performative Time, and Mortuary Space as Locality in the Eastern Iron Age of Southwest Germany* in *Place as Material Culture: Objects, Geographies, and the Construction of Time.* Edited by Dragos Gheorghiu and George Nash. Newcastle-Upon-Tyne, UK: Cambridge Scholars Publications.

Jones, Andrew M. and Benjamin Alberti. 2013. *Archaeology After Interpretation* in *Archaeology After Interpretation.* Benjamin Alberti, Andrew M. Jones, and Joshua Pollard (Editors). Walnut Creek, California: Left Coast Press, Inc. pp. 15-42.

Latour, Bruno. 1996. *On Interobjectivity. Mind, Culture, and Activity 3(4): 228-245.*

Archaeology and Ghost Research: A Relational Entanglement
~ John G. Sabol ~

1999. *Pandora's Hope: Essays on the Reality of Science Studies.* Cambridge, Ma: Harvard University Press.

2005. *ReAssembling the Social: An Introduction to Actor-Network Theory.* Oxford: Oxford University Press.

Lucas, Gavin. 2012. *Understanding the Archaeological Record.* Cambridge: Cambridge University Press.

2013. *Afterword: Archaeology and the Science of New Objects* in *Archaeology After Interpretation.* Benjamin Alberti, Andrew M. Jones, and Joshua Pollard (Editors). Walnut Creek, California: Left Coast Press, Inc. pp. 369-380.

Lucero, Lisa J. 2008. *Memorializing Place Among Classic Maya Commoners* in *Memory Work: Archaeology of Material Practices.* Edited by Barbara J. Mills and William H. Walker. Santa Fe: School for Advanced Research Press. pp. 187-206.

Mathieu, James R. 2002 (Editor). *Experimental Archaeology, Replicating Past Objects, Behaviors, and Processes.* Oxford: BAR International Series 1035.

McLucas, C. 1993. *The Host and the Ghost* (British Gof Archive NLW). Lecture Notes.

Meskell, Lynn. 2002. *Private Life in New Kingdom Egypt.* Princeton: Princeton University Press.

Morgan, R. 1995. *Yllyfyr Glas: British Gof 1988-1995.* Cardiff: Brith Gof.

Moshenska, Gabriel. 2006. *The Archaeological Uncanny. Public Archaeology.* Volume 5:91-99.

Munn, Nancy. 1992. *The Cultural Anthropology of Time: A Critical Essay. Annual Review of Anthropology.* 21: 93-123.

Nader, Laura. 1997. *Law in Culture and Society.* University of California Press.

Olivier, Laurent. 2001. *The Archaeology of the Contemporary Past* in *Archaeologies of the Contemporary Past.* V. Buchli and Gavin Lucas (Editors). London: Routledge. pp.175-188.

2008 (2011). *The Dark Abyss of Time: Archaeology and Memory.* Lanham, California: AltaMira Press.

Pauketat, T.R. 2000. *The Tragedy of the Commoners* in *Agency in Archaeology* Edited by Marcia-Anne Dobres and John Robb. London: Routledge. pp. 113-129.

Pauketat, T.R. and Diana Loren. 2005. *Ancient Cahokia and the Mississippians.* Cambridge: Cambridge University Press.

Pearson, Mike. 2007. *Site-Specific Performance.* (University of Art and Design, Helsinki). Lecture Notes.

2010. *Site-Specific Performance.* New York: Palgrave MacMillian.

Pellegrino, Charles. 2005. *Ghosts of Vesuvius.* New York: Harper Perennial.

Rappaport, Joanne. 1990. *The Politics of Memory: Native Historical Interpretation in the Columbian Andes.* Cambridge: Cambridge University Press.

Sabol, John G. 2014. *Altered States: Making the Extraordinary Ordinary Again.* Bedford, Pa: Ghost Excavation Books, Inc.

Shanks, Michael and Christopher Tilley. 1987. *Re-Constructing Archaeology.* Cambridge: Cambridge University Press.

1993. *Social Theory and Archaeology.* Cambridge: Polity Press.

Shanks, Michael. 2012. *The Archaeological Imagination.* Walnut Creek, California: Left Coast Books, Inc.

Thomas, Julian. 1993. *The Politics of Vision and the Archaeology of Landscape* in *Landscape: Politics and Perspectives.* Barbara Bender (Editor). Oxford: Berg. pp. 19-48.

1996. *Time, Culture, and Identity: An Interpretive Archaeology.* London: Routledge.

Tilley, Christopher. 1989. *Excavation as Theatre. Antiquity* 63 (239): 275-280.

1999. *Metaphor and Material Culture.* London: Berg.

Tuan, Y.F. 1977. *Space and Place: The Perspective of Experience.* Minneapolis: University of Minnesota Press.

Van Gennep, Arnold. 1960. *The Rites of Passage.* Chicago: University of Chicago Press.

Archaeology and Ghost Research: A Relational Entanglement
~ John G. Sabol ~

Vidler, Anthony. 1992. *The Architectural Uncanny*. Cambridge, Ma: MIT Press.

Viveros de Castro, E. 2006. *A Inconstancia de Alma Selvagem*. Sao Paulo: Cosac Nalfy.

Webmoor, Timothy. 2013. *STS, Symmetry, Archaeology* in *The Oxford Handbook of the Contemporary World*. Edited by Paul Graves-Brown, Rodney Harrison, and Angela Piccini. Oxford: Oxford University Press. pp. 105-120.

Williams, Raymond. 1977. *Marxism and Literature*. Oxford: Oxford University Press.

Witmore, Christopher. 2007. *Landscape, Time, Topography: An Archaeological Account of the Southern Argolid, Greece* in *Envisioning Landscape, Situations, and Standpoints in Archaeology and Heritage*. D. Hicks, L. McAtackney, and G. Fairclough (Editors). Walnut Creek, California: Left Coast Press, Inc. pp. 194-225.

2009. *Prolegomena to Open Pasts: On Archaeological Memory Practices*. Archaeologies: Journal of the World Archaeological Congress. Vol. 5, No. 3: 511-545.

Wlodarski, Robert and Anne Wlodarski. 1997. *The Haunted Whaley House: San Diego, California*. Lava Place, West Hills, California: G-Host Publishing.

Wooffitt, Robin. 2010. *Towards a Sociological Parapsychology* in *Anomalous Experiences: Essays from Parapsychology and*

Psychological Perspectives. Edited by Matthew D. Smith. Jefferson, North Carolina: McFarland and Co. pp. 72-92.

Zimmerman, Larry J. 2001. *Usurping Native American Voice* in *The Future of the Past: Archaeology, North America, and Repatriation.* Tamara I. Bray (Editor). New York: Garland Publishing. Pp. 169-184.

Archaeology and Ghost Research: A Relational Entanglement
~ John G. Sabol ~

Author's Biography

Photo 20: Photo of the Author, John Sabol

John Sabol is an archaeologist, cultural anthropologist, actor, and author. As an archaeologist, he has unearthed past material remains in excavations and site surveys in England, Mexico, and at various sites in the United States (including Eastern South Dakota, the Tennessee River Valleys, and in Pennsylvania). His anthropological fieldwork includes the studies of "spirits" in the religious beliefs of the afterlife among various cultural groups in Mexico (Mixtec, Zapotec, Lacandon, Nahuatl, and Otomi). His acting career includes "ghosting" performances of

Archaeology and Ghost Research: A Relational Entanglement
~ John G. Sabol ~

various characters and scenarios in more than 35 movies, TV shows, and documentaries. He has appeared in the A&E TV series, Paranormal State as an investigative consultant.

He has written twenty-one books. These include: ***Ghost Excavator (2007), Ghost Culture (2007), Gettysburg Unearthed (2007), Battlefield Hauntscape (2008), The Anthracite Coal Region: The Archaeology of its Haunting Presence (2008), The Politics of Presence: Haunting Performances on the Gettysburg Battlefield (2008), Bodies of Substance, Fragments of Memories: An Archaeological Sensitivity to Ghostly Presence (2009), Phantom Gettysburg (2009), Digging Deep: An Archaeologist Unearths a Haunted Life (2009), The Re-Hauntings of Gettysburg (2010), Digging Up Ghosts (2011), The Haunted Theatre (2011), Haunting Archaeologies (2012), Beyond the Paranormal: Unearthing An Extended "Normal" at Haunted Locations (2013), Burnside Bridge Hauntscape: The Excavation of a Civil War Soundscape (2013), The Gettysburg Battlefield Experience (2013), The Good Death and The Civil War (2014), Centralia: A Vision of Ruin (2014), Altered States: Making the Extraordinary Ordinary Again.***

His recent speaking engagements include the T.A.G. (Theoretical Archaeology Group) Conference at the University of California, Berkeley, at the Space and Place Conference in Prague, Czech Republic, the TAG

Archaeology and Ghost Research: A Relational Entanglement
~ John G. Sabol ~

Conference at the University in Buffalo, New York, Exploring the Extraordinary Conference in York, England, the C.H.A.T. archaeological conference also in York, and the GHost Conference at the University of London, London, England.

His investigative reports have been published in such diverse venues as Haunted Times Magazine, Tennessee Anthropologist, and the online journal, ParaAnthropology. He has been a frequent guest on numerous radio and internet talk shows, among them, Beyond the Edge Radio, The Paranormal View, Para X Radio, Blog Talk Radio, The Grand Dark Conspiracy, and Rusty O'Nhiall's "Mysterious and Unexplained" on PsiFM (Australia). He was a university professor in Mexico for 11 years, teaching both undergraduate and graduate courses on the anthropology of tourism. He has also been featured on public educational TV for U.S. and foreign markets, and has worked on international educational documentaries (in Spain).

He has a M.A. in Anthropology/Archaeology (University of Tennessee), and a B.A. in Sociology/Anthropology (Bloomsburg University). He has also attended Penn State University, the University of Pittsburgh, the University of the Americas (Cholula, Puebla, Mexico), and has studied theatre and method acting in Mexico City.

He can be reached via email at cuicospirit@hotmail.com. His website is: **www.ghostexcavation.com** and he can be found on Facebook ("Ghost Excavations with John Sabol").

Made in the USA
Charleston, SC
29 July 2014